MW01205582

Better Out Than In

In

Book I

By

Sylvia Cooper

This book is dedicated to my wonderful husband, Allan Cooper, who is truly my partner and best friend. To my son Chris Roots who has always been my champion. To my beautiful daughter, Chardonnay, who fills my heart with laughter and love. To my thoughtful and generous daughter-in-law, Polina Roots. To my sister Rosemary Kombo who saw me through it all. And lastly but certainly not least, Regina Melvin who read through every iteration and encouraged me through to publication. To all of you, many thanks. I love you.

CooperLand Publishing: Sugar Land, Texas © 2017
Copyright 2017 All Rights Reserved © 2017
ISBN: 978-0-9987 162-0-6
ISBN: 978-0-9987 162-1-3

Table of Contents

Prologue

Before I opened my mouth to take a bite, he stood looking me up and down with disgust written on his face. Spittle had collected in the corners of his mouth. He snatched the plate of food from my hands and flung it across the room, knocking my favorite red ceramic Chinese vase off the wooden coffee table. It had been a wedding present from my mother. There was a spine-tingling crash as the fragments flew like a thousand sparkling fireflies, flying in all directions, across the dark wooden floor. The plate landed on the glass display cabinet covering the front door with thick brown gravy. At that moment, I felt my legs and hands shaking like I had a traumatic brain injury. I told myself to run for my life. My lips and chin quivered as my heart pounded nearly detonating. Trembling, I hobbled to the kitchen. I heard footsteps and I smelled his cologne. I knew he was coming after me.

"You liar, you think you can play games with me bitch?"

Chapter 1: No Excuse

Domestic violence is nothing new especially in my culture. I am from Zimbabwe. My country of origin is located in southern Africa, between the Zambezi and Limpopo Rivers. It is bordered by South Africa to the south, Botswana to the west and southwest, Zambia to the northwest, and Mozambique to the east and northeast. While it is landlocked, there are many beautiful rivers and a smattering of lakes. It's a beautiful country but marred by the heinous human rights violations.

Domestic violence is not considered a "human rights" violation per say but it is certainly a violation committed against women and children daily. Almost half (47%) of the women in Zimbabwe endure gender-based violence usually at the hands of their husbands. Sadly, a study done by a local university showed 30% of women interviewed felt that men had a right to beat their wives and almost 100% of men. My first husband, Dracul, was no exception.

Violence against women, as the studies show, is very common. My experience with beatings started long before I married Dracul; it started when I was a child; my siblings and I watching my father beat my mother. It was frightening to hear his fists on her flesh and to see the horrible bruises it left. It was a sight and sound that would remain with me for years to come. It never occurred to me at the time that I would one day be in the same horrible nightmare.

Chapter 2: The Beginning

My half-sister, Evelyn, and I were seven years apart. When I got married, I was ecstatic and hoped to live walking distance from her. How I convinced my ex-husband to live that close to her is still a mystery to me. I watched my sister's relationship with her husband; he kissed her good-bye every morning before leaving for work, he would often pick up food after work so she wouldn't have to cook. Her living room was always filled with the flowery scent from her favorite red roses he brought home just because he wanted to. I wanted a marriage like hers.

My marriage was far from the story-book one Evelyn had. The abuse began and my sister gave me strength while giving me a shoulder to cry on but she felt helpless. Powerless to help me after having seen the results of my husband's beating. I had run to her countless times

with battered faces looking like I had been in a

championship boxing match and clearly lost. I was

emotionally drained and physically exhausted.

CHAPTER 3: The Early Years

I was born in 1967 to a middle-class family and grew up in a township called Kambuzuma in Harare. I lived a relatively average life for the most part. My parents, Jonah and Sarah, were hard workers who believed in educating their children. Despite the hard work, my parents always had smiles on their faces. The work was hard, but it was grand.

Our home was not large. It was far from adequate for the at least ten people who occupied it, but we were grateful for it. We always had cousins, uncles or some distant relative living with us. The house was comprised of mum and dad's bedroom, the girl's bedroom, the boy's bedroom, living room, dining room and a kitchen. The house was one story, painted sky blue with an average front yard to play in. My parents had purchased the land and built the house. There was no such thing as mortgage, loans or credit cards in 1960's Africa. You had to save your money and buy what you wanted or needed.

Come to think of it now, that is why my parents were never financially stressed. Because everything was paid for in cash, there was no chance of going into debt like there is nowadays. It was a cool way of living. Basically, if you could not pay cash for it, you could not afford it period.

A month shy my 6th birthday, my little sister, Elizabeth (Betty as we call her), was born. I was no longer dad's one and only little girl. This made me jealous. I watched my dad rocking her in her crib and I would ask, "Dad am I still your number one girl?

He smiled, "Of course, you will always be and your sister is my number two."

I remember sitting on my dad's lap and he would tickle my neck with his beard making me laugh hysterically. When my little sister was born, I considered her as a trespasser. It was no longer dad and me. Now my sister was always part of the equation. When my sister was three and I about eight, dad used to make us sit on his lap. He would tickle us both with his beard.

Dad would come home with a bottle of Coca-Cola and my siblings and I would line up with plastic tumblers in one hand and he would share the Coca-Cola with six of us. When he ate, he would share his food with us too.

We did not have a television or electronic gadgets to entertain us growing up so, most of our time was spent outdoors. One of my neighbors down my street was the first to buy a television. They would leave the curtains open and let the kids from the street watch television from their veranda. The veranda would be teeming with kids. I remember we would watch Maniac and Cabaret starring Liza Minnelli and Michael York. By the time I was a teenager, my father and most of the families on our street, had televisions.

One of my childhood memories is my mother sitting at her Singer sewing machine, on the veranda making clothes. She would go away for a few days every month to a small city outside Harare called Kadoma- Chakari Mine to sell the clothes she made. Kadoma is about 145 kilometers from Harare.

My occupation as a child was to play. It was like work for me. I was kind of a loner as a little girl, happy playing with my dolls. One afternoon I was playing with my dolls in our front garden in my mother's view. "Sylvie come here. Let me get rid of a bug on your back."

I heard the word bug, and I went insane. Instead of going to my mom, I started sprinting around the house screaming and crying, at the same time trying to take off the yellow t-shirt I had on.

"Come here. What are you doing?" Mom said.

I went around the house again still crying. I was scared and I could not believe that the bug was on my back. As I came around the corner, my mom was waiting for me. She grabbed me, and demanded I calm down. After that, she simply flicked the bug off my back with scissors.

My father came home from work two days after the bug incident. He wore brown overalls and black working boots, carrying a bag of treats for my brothers and me.

"Daddy, daddy," I ran into his arms.

He had gone to Bulawayo to make some deliveries for work. My mom was waiting eagerly to tell him about the bug drama. I remember everyone laughing at the dinner table, and I laughed with them. When it comes to bugs, I haven't changed since then.

This incident remains vivid in my mind; despite that I was only five years old. I remember my mother laughing uncontrollably every time she told the story. My mom was a person who was easily amused anyway, she laughed all the time.

My mother most often wore a floral knee length dress, which showed her curvaceous frame, with a matching head wrap. Considering she was in her late thirties with eleven children, she looked amazing. Her marriage to my father was her second marriage. She had had five children in her first marriage. With my father, she had Wellington and Edwin, twins older than me, Edgar, 11 months older than me, I was next then Stanford, and Elizabeth who were both younger than me.

~~~~

Anna and Bread

I heard the brass school bell sound ding-dong, ding-dong sound, immediately followed by the teacher's high pitched voice, "Class is dismissed, have a good weekend."

I raced home and heard mom talking to someone in the living room. I went to find out and it was Anna our new maid. Mom had told my siblings and me that Anna was arriving that afternoon. Mom also said that she was an orphan who was raised by an aunt. Unfortunately, her aunt was tormenting her physically and emotionally and that she wanted to work to free herself from the abuse. I looked across the room at her and wondered if this was true.

At nine, I was almost same height as Anna, which I liked because I believed I had a new friend. She was short and stout with anime brown eyes. Her teeth were crooked, lower slanted back as if someone had furiously knocked them in. Sis Anna (as we called her) oversaw the household, including my siblings and me when my parents were out of town on business.

It didn't take long for Anna to find out that I was a bed wetter. I wet the bed at least every other day and mom always used to say I would grow out of it. Anna waited for my mother to go on one of her trips and she made one rule. No drinks, including water, in the evenings. This rule was for me only and was enforced when my parents were away. It was intended to stop me from wetting my bed. I recall one night I went to bed uncomfortably thirsty. Sneaking in and out of the kitchen unnoticed, I quietly fumbled around searching for a water tumbler which I knew was in the cabinet beside the stove. As I reached for the glass, I retreated in fear so fast one would have thought the glass was made from prickly brush and had pierced my fingertips.

Some mornings I dreaded waking up feeling embarrassed and ashamed realizing that I had wet my bed. The first day alone with Anna, I wet my bed. She grabbed me by the arm, dragged me into the shower with the water turned all the way to cold. It sent shivers down my spine as my body numbed and tensed up with the first drops of freezing water on my skin. Breathing heavily as the cold water ran down my shivering body, she scrubbed my back and butt like she was scrubbing a contaminated hospital floor. She would remind me not to ever wet the bed again.

Every morning, Anna would buy a loaf of fresh Lobels white bread. The bread man would come around, riding a tricycle, with a yellow and green metal box with words written in big letters, "Lobels Bread", shouting "baker ambuya, baker ambuya." Meaning, your bread man is here. The bread man's voice would send my brother and me into hysteria mode rushing to get to the kitchen table first, to earn the heel of the bread. This was another one of Anna's rules—whoever got to the table first, got the heel of the bread. Edgar and I were eleven months apart. He was older but we were both obsessed with the heel of the bread. It was almost certain that Edgar and I would have a fight over the heel of the loaf every morning.

As a girl, I took longer to get ready for school which was a huge advantage for my brother. He beat me to the table often resulting in me missing out on the coveted heel of the bread. No matter how much I tried to compromise or argue with Anna, I could not convince her otherwise. It was her way or highway. As usual, my brother beat me to it one morning and I decided to do something about it. I reached for his plate and snatched his heel of the bread. He screamed at me to put it back. Anna came to his rescue also demanding that I put it back. I started eating the bread. My brother got up from his chair and pounced on me, knocking me off my chair. All that time Anna just stood there like a dummy, rubbing it in.

"Why did you take his bread? You deserve a good beating," she said.

I tried to defend myself which made my brother angrier punching me harder. That day he kicked my butt, and this would mark our last physical fight. I knew then that he was getting stronger than me.

Still, sitting at that four-chair, patterned acrylic red and white kitchen table (matching the red and white floor tiles) in the corner of the room facing the window, where my four brothers and I would have breakfast every morning, is a wonderful memory. We would watch Anna standing next to a white, four plate stove, which was to our left, side slicing bread with her back to us. The bread was freshly baked and still so warm that when you spread butter on it, it would melt. The smell of freshly baked Lobels bread was mouthwatering. I have not come across tasty bread like I ate every morning before going to school during my childhood. I would go back to those good old days to eat that bread again.

CHAPTER 4: Step-Monster

These happy memories would soon be tarnished, when my father married Judith his second wife. On reflection, half of my childhood was perfect and the other half was horrible.

I was just a kid but I remember very well how my father started seeing Judith behind my mother's back. To earn extra money, women from Kambuzuma and Mufakose would ride-share back and forth to Mbare market in my dad's van for a fee. Sometimes my father would take my sister, brother and me to Mbare on Saturdays. During these trips to Mbare, my father met Judith. She lived in Mufakose with her parents and had just divorced her first husband.

I believe my mother found out about Judith from one of the ladies. There was an incident where I was in the car with my mother and dad was driving. They started arguing about Judith. My father said to my mother if she wanted to confront Judith, he would take her to Judith's place. He increased the speed going past the turn to our house. My mother told him to stop and that she did not want to go to Judith's place. My father continued driving. I remember my mother opening the door of the car and jumping out while the car was still moving. Lucky enough, there were no cars behind us otherwise she could have been run over.

I cried hysterically because I thought my mother was going to die. My mother was then taken to the nearest clinic where the abrasions to her knees and elbows were cleaned and dressed. My mother was lucky that her injuries were minor. Thinking about it now, I wonder what was going through her mind at that time—was she not ready to face Judith?

After a few months, the affair got serious and my father finally informed my mother that he was going to marry a second wife; Judith. Polygamy was common in Africa in the 70s. It was not a big deal for a man to have more than one wife. Obviously, it was a big deal to my mother because she now had to share her husband with another woman. Judith moved in with us, but she had her room at the back of the house. It was more like a studio flat.

A few months after Judith moved in, mother was standing by the stove cooking beef for dinner. Father walked into the kitchen and confronted mother about rumors she was spreading about Judith being a home wrecker. My mother responded to the effect that she was indeed a gold digger. Father got mad and I heard a loud smacking sound as he slapped mother across the face. I looked at my big brothers who were sitting at the kitchen table with me in horror and fear. Father grabbed mother by the hair dragging her into their bedroom where he continued to beat her up.

The kitchen started filling up with the smell of burning meat and smoke from the pan on the stove. One of my brothers turned the stove off.

My brother hugged me as we stood outside the bedroom door. Crying, I started banging on the door asking father to stop beating mother. This went on for what seemed like forever. When it was over, I snuggled under my blanket begging for God to stop father from beating mother again. Unfortunately, this was the start of uncountable beatings my mother would receive from father.

Despite my parent's marriage being rocky, in 1975 my mother had her seventh child with my father; my baby brother Prosper. It was as if my mother had signed up for some rapid growing countries competition, and she was being loyal to her country.

One afternoon when I was about eleven, my mother surprised my siblings and me by announcing that we were moving to Waterfalls, a low-density area. That was definitely an upgrade from Kambuzuma. We were excited because in those days not a lot of black families lived in low density areas. Although the word divorce was never mentioned, I believe my mother had checked out of her marriage.

The first day we moved, my siblings and I went insane. "Ooh look, we have a sink in the kitchen," I yelled.

In Kambuzuma the sink was outside. My mother had instilled a hard work ethic in me and as a girl I had to learn to do housework at an early age. At eleven, I was already doing dishes, sweeping, mopping and polishing floors. I remember when learning to iron, I tried to stand the iron up on the ironing board; it flipped back on my right hand burning me. I still have scars to remind me.

Down the hallway, I heard Stanford screaming, "We have a bathtub, this is so cool!"

This house was everything that the Kambuzuma house wasn't. For the first time, I got my own room. It was about the size of a prison cell but my single bed and a bookcase fit nicely. Beetroot colored carpet, pink walls (which I couldn't wait to cover with Michael Jackson posters).

The new house did not make our life any easier. My father refused to help mother financially. Shortly after moving in, things started getting tougher for mom. She couldn't afford to pay for the house and the bills. In an attempt to help mother, my two young brothers, Stanford, Prosper and I, resorted to shoplifting. We didn't shop lift for clothes but food; mainly frozen whole chickens. I don't remember whose idea it was, but we did it three or four times without getting caught.

One Saturday evening, my brothers and I went on our mission to steal frozen chicken. Upon entering the store, we headed to the back of the shop to the deep freezers section. Next to the chicken freezer was a fish freezer, but we had decided that the smell of the fish could get us caught so we left the fish alone. Stanford, covering for us, distracted the shop assistant by buying a few candies. Prosper opened the fridge and picked two whole chickens dropping them one at a time, after scanning the area to be sure the coast was clear, into the plastic bag that I had ready opened. Unfortunately, we didn't realize we were being watched.

As we started walking towards the exit, I was grabbed from the back. "Hey! Did you pay for that?" Asked, the shop assistant. I tried to free myself from his grip but it felt like he had industrial super glue in his hand. The feeling you get in sleep paralysis, you are awake and you feel like you are being held down, you can't move or scream. I froze. The tremors in my hands and fingers were obvious as the bag with the chicken started rustling like plastic wrap. My brothers shot out of the shop leaving me behind. "Put it back," the man demanded. He was a tall big fat man, stinking of alcohol and cigarette smoke. Shaking, I walked back to the fridge and emptied the contents into the freezer. I turned around and noticed the man raising his right hand. He threw it forward as hard and as fast as he could, slapping me across the face. It stung, and for a moment I saw flecks of uniformed light. "If I ever catch you again, I will call the police on you. Leave now!" he shouted. I zoomed out of the store. That would mark the end of stealing frozen chicken.

A few months later my mother discovered that raising seven children on her own was not as easy as she thought. She decided to disappear from it all. One weekend my father came to pick my siblings and me up to meet our grandmother who had arrived a day before from the village. Mom discouraged me from going and I stayed. She had planned her escape from the stress and my father. As soon as my father left, a truck came to pick us up along with a few pieces of furniture. Mother dropped the house keys at the landlord's office on our way to Kadoma.

We moved to Kadoma leaving behind my five brothers and sister. This was not my mother's first rodeo. She had left her five children behind from her first marriage. I met four of them when I was about five; Immaculate, Maxwell, Beauty and Evelyn. In fact, Evelyn lived with us for a few years before she got married.

I remember how Evelyn was fond of me as a little girl. She did my hair, painted my nails and took me everywhere with her. She got married at an early age. I remember a few months into her marriage, she asked me to have a sleep over at her apartment and I made up a lie. I told her mom and dad had said no. I did not want her husband to know that I wet my bed. Not accepting this, she decided to confront Mom. Mom said, "Of course she can come spend a night with her big sis." I knew then that my unpleasant curse was not going to be a secret anymore.

I was not worried about my sister, because she already knew that I was a bed wetter, it was her husband. I must have been about nine years old and there was no sign that I was going to stop wetting the bed soon. My fears would be confirmed the next morning. I woke up and felt the warmth underneath, I knew I had just peed, I could smell it and my pajamas were soaking wet. I lay there imagining what Jacob was going to think about me. *"A nine-year-old girl, still peeing in bed, that's gross,"* I thought. I became very anxious and I knew I had to do something. *Wait till sis wakes up and tell her, don't say anything and just make the bed with soaked sheets, or disappear.* I decided to disappear and walked back home. Thankfully she didn't live far from my house. After a few hours, she came looking for me. That's when I told her that I was embarrassed that I wet the bed. She tried to convince me to go back to her house but I refused.

Isadora was my other half-brother that I had never met. The story was that he moved to Zambia as a teenager. Until now, I don't know why my mom decided to take me with her and not my baby brother.

We had been in Kadoma for less than six months when my father hunted us down and brought us back to Harare. Looking back now, Judith must have put pressure on my father to find mother because she didn't want to raise another woman's children. At that time my mother was like a fireman—only needed when there were life threatening signs. This time we would move to his new house in Glen View. I was happy to be reunited with my siblings.

Although my parents were not in a relationship, I remember dad beating mom a few times again in Glen View. Mother had moved on and was seeing someone. The problem was that she was living in my dad's house and he was not happy with the arrangement. Mother's affair got serious and she had a child with another man, a baby girl, and baby number thirteen. It reminds me of the reality show Nineteen Kids and Counting. To be, fair mother was so desperate for father to get out of her life, she was willing to do anything. Let's face it, her attempt to move to another town, Kadoma, failed. She knew better, disappearing was not an option. The chances were he would hunt her down again and find her. She took a drastic measure by getting pregnant by another man to send a message to my father that left no room for interpretation—she was finished with him for good.

The winter I was fourteen, my mother left for good. Looking back, the situation must have been like a cow giving birth to twins. My mother's new man did not want anything to do with another man's children. Mother had to choose between him or my siblings and me; she chose him. My siblings and I returned to Kambuzuma again where we would live under the rules set down by Judith.

~~~

ALONE WITH JUDITH

The second week after we moved in, that Monday morning my father went out of town on a business trip. Dinner time my family and I sat at a solid wood dining room table, near a window that looked out on the neighbor's house. Edgar sat beside me while Judith sat across him. Judith had piled a ton of food on his plate. I recall that Judith had been upset that Edgar would go to my father complaining that he was still hungry and father would give him half of his food. Edgar was a big eater. The mountain of food was enough for four of us. As he began to eat, her hands closed into fists as she crouched forward and demanded that he eat everything on his plate. She watched him like a hawk keeping a brown leather belt threateningly beside her. We thought her eyes would burst into flames at the angry look she directed at Edgar.

It was quiet except for the sound Edgar made chowing down his food. I noticed my little brother's eyes were watery, enlarged and his hands trembled as he picked up a glass of water. He did not like belts. Edgar ate as much as he could and then he said he had enough. Judith motioned him to continue eating. I offered to help him but she gave me a look and I knew she meant 'don't you dare'. I looked at Edgar and his eyes were moist. I wanted to comfort him but I felt helpless. I knew then that my siblings and I, like Cinderella, had acquired a wicked stepmother.

Prosper, another younger brother, left the table and I followed him to his room where he sat crouched in a corner, tears rolling down his chubby cheeks. Trying to hold my own tears, I motioned to him to stand up and gently hugged him as he put his head on my shoulder. I assured him that everything was going to be fine. No sooner had I reassured him, smacking sounds came from the kitchen followed by Edgar's scream. Then there was a sound of a stack of books falling off the bookshelf as Edgar bolted from Judith as fast as he could. I dashed into the dining room to see what was going on, and he almost knocked me over as he ran out of the house.

On another occasion as I sat slumped in a chair, my hand on my throat, I watched Judith destroying my 6-year-old brother's toy car (a present from our aunt), because he did not stop making engine sounds as he played, after she asked him to stop for the second time. Hammering away, the toy car looked like it had gone through a scrap car shredder. Noticing his eyes tearing up, I pulled him into a side hug while I rubbed his back.

The following week I witnessed destruction of yet another thing that mattered to my little brother, a makeshift football that my elder brother made for him. I heard the snip of the scissors repeatedly as she cut the ball into pieces. I felt heaviness in my chest and limbs as my brother begged her to stop. This time he did not follow house rules, no playing ball in the house.

It was a winter evening; I was hanging out with my brothers and their friends by the fire in the backyard. Our neighbors were doing the same, sitting by the fire. Although we could not see each other because of the red brick wall between our gardens, we could hear each other and easily had a conversation. We were roasting maize on the cob, our favorite snack. The aroma of roasted maze mixed with the burning wood filled the air. The loud popping and hissing as it roasted, turning to a golden yellow and black color served as a reminder to keep any eye on the roasted maze so it didn't burn.

Judith decided to come to the back garden. She started talking to the neighbor over the wall. Laughing sarcastically, she said, "I did not give anyone's mother a pass to sleep around."

I looked at my older brother and without saying a word we knew that she was referring to our mother. I was sitting on a log and felt my nostrils flaring, my mouth quivering and drooling. My heart rate increased and my muscles tensed up. The urge to fight her was getting stronger and stronger. I wanted to jump on her and punch her until I couldn't. I pulled myself together and went to the restroom where I broke down.

While I was in the restroom I heard my father's hoarse voice as he arrived home from work. I washed my face with cold water so that no one would notice that I had been crying, including my father. I thought about what would happen to my brothers the next time he went out of town if he knew why I was crying; especially to Prosper. I had learned that sucking it up was the way to go after what happened to Edgar. In fact, my father was not aware of the first incident. My brothers and I agreed that it was best not to say anything because we believed we were protecting the younger siblings from abuse. My older brothers and I would spend the day in school most times fearing for our little brother.

Judith kept many things locked away from us. Snacks such as cookies, candy and sodas and luxury items such as perfumed soaps, body lotions, perfume sprays and deodorant were some of her special treasures. The only person who had access to the keys was my half-sister, Judith's eldest daughter with my dad, who was about eleven years old that time. Every time my half-sister walked past, I heard the jangling of keys hanging around her neck. She always smelled like fresh flowers after taking a shower and I would ask her if I could borrow her moisturizer and deodorant but she would always say she did not have any or she had run out.

At fifteen years old, physical appearance and fitting in was very important to me. Because personal hygiene items were kept locked away by Judith and my half-sister, I found myself forced to improvise when it came to personal care. At times, I would make butter, or any cooking oil, work as moisturizer leaving me with a crayon, putty smell. My mother had always given me Nivea cream when I was with her but now I was forced to use butter or cooking oil as a moisturizer. I could never tell my father out of fear of consequences of physical violence from Judith.

~~~

TSORO GAME

As a teenager, I became very close to my siblings. In Harare's climate, which is very close to perfect if not perfect, my brothers and I spent most evenings in our cousin Vivian's (Vee as I call her) back garden hanging out with her and her brothers playing draughts, morris (tsoro yemutwelve). The game is played by two people at a time. We dug holes, and they would be divided equally among the two players and filled with equal number of stones. The idea was to pick a hole that is used as a bank to store all the stones in the other holes. The first player to fill his bank hole wins the game. It's a very strategic game. If you were really good, you would fill your bank hole without giving the other player an opportunity to play. The game is very entertaining and usually played by boys.

Vivian and I spent most of the nights watching our brothers play. Vivian was my aunt's only daughter and was a few years older than me. Like me she had four brothers. Her oldest brother used to win all the time so I decided to focus on him each night he played. After observing him play for about two weeks, I realized that he always started from the same hole and that would not give the other player chance to play. Equipped with this information, one night it dawned on me that I could actually play.

"I want to be next," I demanded.

"I will knock her out in one go, it will not take a minute," one of my cousin boosted.

"Can I go first?" I asked.

Laughing the boys said, "Sure," in tandem.

Using my cousin's strategy, I won my first tsoro game without giving the other player a chance to play. With her eyes as big as quarters, Vee asked, "How did you do it?"

I would play Tsoro for hours at times, sometimes until early hours of the morning. I played this game and outdid my brothers, cousins and their friends. No females would participate in this game, however being the only girl in the family at that time, I had no choice but to play with my brothers. It became one of my favorite things to do with my siblings. It brought us a closeness that we had not shared before.

Chapter 5: Meeting Dracul

I entered the kitchen using the back door. The table was to my right and next to the table was a kitchen sink and opposite of the sink was a stove. Vee was standing by the stove cooking. I took my shoes off and walked barefoot, the grey and white tiles freezing cold on my feet. Vee offered me her house shoes and I graciously accepted. As I sat, a young man walked into the kitchen from the living room almost hitting his head on the door head.

"Hi Uncle," Vee said.

"It smells good in here, what are you cooking?" he asked reaching for a chair.

He spoke with a heavy Masvingo dialect. I noticed his khaki shirt wet with perspiration under his arms. He pulled the waist band of his faded Levis, and sat revealing his brown shoes. Vee introduced him as her mother's brother. Per my culture, it made him my uncle too.

"Do you live around here?" turning towards me, he asked.

"She lives down the road," Vee said before I answered.

He talked to Vee for a few minutes and went back into the living room where my aunt was knitting while watching one of her favorite shows, Dynasty.

I sat on Vee's veranda the following day helping her undo her braids, she announced that her Uncle Dracul was interested in me with a wide grin. Jerking my head back with my mouth falling open, I felt a sudden chill at my core. Although my aunt was not blood related to my father, I found it awkward that my aunt's brother would be interested in me and Vee appeared fine with it.

Later that day my aunt confirmed what Vee had told me earlier about Dracul. This time I was puzzled. I was hearing this from my confidant. I was lost for words. I asked her to repeat what she had just said. I must admit, I did find him attractive and charming, but every time I thought about him, my whole body would overheat and I had butterflies in my stomach. Little did I know then that an apple can be great on the outside but not so great on the inside.

Before long we were dating secretly. I was scared to death of brothers, especially when it came to dating. Then there was my father, who need not say anything but just gave me that look.

After few weeks dating on a Sunday evening, I agreed to stop by Dracul's place believing he just wanted to pick something up before heading to the shops. Instead he forced me to have sex.

"If we were boyfriend and girlfriend, you would want to make me happy wouldn't you?" he asked. "What kind of a girlfriend who does not want to make her boyfriend happy?" he continued.

"This is wrong. I am not ready to do this. I have never had sex and I believed in sex after marriage," I protested.

He ignored me and used force to keep me down. Powerless against his strength, I felt 'disconnected' as he attacked me. I couldn't comprehend what was happening to me. Dracul was renting a room two blocks from my house. His landlord was friends with my father. Screaming was not an option for me. The last thing I wanted was for my father and brothers find out that I was alone with this older man in his room.

As I walked home I muttered to myself, *"What have I done, how could I let this happen?"* When I got home, I went straight to my room, threw myself on the bed, and punched fists against my thighs as I let out an involuntary moan.

Six weeks later, one morning as I walked to the kitchen, I heard bacon sizzling in the pan and it smelled like crispy barbeque. The smell got strong as I walked into the kitchen, sending me to the restroom to throw up. I found myself struggling with the smell and decided to go to Vee's house.

Vee's favorite perfume smelled like strawberry and chocolate and the smell lasted all day. She had let me use her perfume many times and I loved it. But on this day when I entered Vee's bedroom while she was getting dressed, the same perfume made me sick. I dashed to the restroom to throw up.

That night as I lie on my bed, I wondered why the smell of bacon and Vee's perfume bothered me earlier. Then it occurred to me that my uterus ninjas had not visited for over a month now. I felt heavy and numb and my mouth went dry. I could be pregnant, dang it! This was my worst nightmare. I felt hurt and was angry at Dracul. I cried myself to sleep. The rest of the week I had nausea, excessive sweating and, at times, tingling in my chest. I avoided my siblings as well as my Aunt Rhoda and Vee.

Three weeks went by and the symptoms were getting worse. I decided to tell Aunt Rhoda. She was sitting outside on her veranda knitting as usual. "Good afternoon Aunt," I said as I approached her.

"Good afternoon amainini," meaning niece she responded.

As I sat next to her she looked at me and asked, "Are you alright? Your eyes are so puffy. Have you been crying?"

I started tearing up and in seconds I was a complete mess.

Squeezing my hand, she said, "You are not alone. What it is that is bothering you?"

Avoiding eye contact and biting my nails I said, "I think I am pregnant."

I noticed her pinching the skin at her throat and biting her bottom lip before she said, "You are pregnant. It is Dracul's isn't it? How am I going to tell your father?"

Hearing her words, I felt the hairs on the back of my neck stand up.

She sent Vee to find Dracul at the shops where he was drinking beer with friends. On Dracul's arrival, she did not waste time breaking the news to him. She demanded he do the right thing, accept responsibility and marry me. To my surprise, Dracul took it lightly and said he was taking full responsibility and he would inform the rest of his family. With my eyes closed, I let my head fall back. *"One more problem to go,'* I thought, *"my father."*

My father sat on the chair in the living room across from my aunt, directing his gaze at her. Although they were not biologically related, they had been calling each other brother and sister for over twenty years, sharing special occasions such as weddings, graduations and family gatherings. Now she felt like an accomplice and could not look at him. She kept patting the sofa cushion and shifting position. Clearly, she did not want to give him the news, and he wasn't about to make it easy for her. He remained silent, waiting getting up only to straighten a picture or two that hung on the wall.

Aunt cleared her throat for the millionth time. "Brother, you are going to be a grandfather, and the man involved wants to do the right thing. He wants to marry Sylvia".

Father leaped to his feet knocking the glass of water off the coffee table. It sailed across the living room spilling its content on her as he stormed out of the living

room. He obviously had not seen this coming.

Chapter 6: Meeting the In-Laws

Dracul's eldest brother and father figure, Jimmy, had to approve of me before we could be married and he wanted to meet me. The problem was he lived in Bulawayo, Zimbabwe's second largest city some 366 kilometers from Harare. The thought of asking my father's permission to make this journey made my insides quiver. Aunt once again came to my rescue and offered to talk to father. To my surprise he agreed.

"You can go meet his family, but it does not mean that I am agreeing to you getting married," father had warned.

Seizing the opportunity before it melted away, Dracul made the travel arrangements for mid-April 1986. Vee was to travel with us. It was my first time on the train. The locomotives were brown at the top and bottom and beige in the middle, with big letters N.R.Z, which stands for National Railways of Zimbabwe. We were still using the Garratt locomotive steam engine at the time.

I boarded the train and was immediately overwhelmed by the staggering stench of alcohol in the economy coach. Vee and I sat by the window facing each other and Dracul sat next to me. There were drunkards sitting behind us talking, and sometimes singing incessantly until finally they fell asleep. If the drunkards weren't enough, a woman sat behind Vee with her four children hollering, screaming and fighting, or being generally an annoyance. It made for a long ride.

Getting off the train on that wet cool day in April, the station was stuffed with travelers either getting off the train or waiting for trains. We maneuvered our way by identifying small gaps between people and squeezing through. I was glad when we got into a taxi.

Driving through the city headed to Jimmy's place, I noticed that Bulawayo City was similar to Harare City. The outskirts appeared ancient and as we drove through the city center the buildings were more modern. It was rush hour as people were going to work, so it took us almost an hour to get to Jimmy's place in one of Bulawayo suburbs.

The taxi pulled up to the gate at Jimmy's house and tooted few times announcing our arrival. The house was a one story big L-Shaped painted green, surrounded by a chain-link fence. A young lady came out running and unlocked the chain-link double gate. She wore a black dress with white apron and a cap. Her shoes looked like nurse type of shoes. The driver pulled into the cracked concrete drive over run with weeds growing from the cracks.

We entered the house through the front French doors that opened into the living room featuring large brown couches and a nice dark wood coffee table. We were greeted by the familiar fragrance of fried eggs wafting from the kitchen. I was in the first trimester of my pregnancy and as most women do, had cravings for particular foods. In my case, fried eggs. The smell of the eggs cooking stirred the voices in my head, "go get some, go get some, go get some," they repeated.

It was customary to remove your shoes when entering a home and I could not wait to kick mine off. I walked across the living room feeling the warm hardwood floors on my bare feet. I found a chair that faced a large window overlooking the back garden and sat. The garden had several mature avocado, lemon and orange trees loaded with fruit. There was also a children's play area with a swing next to a large area lush with olive green grass.

The children were off to school when we arrived. When they returned, Dracul introduced each of them. The children were of all ages and I quickly lost track of names and ages. Jimmy had ten children with four different women including his current wife Gigi.

Jimmy and Gigi returned that evening after closing their shops. He wore a black suit and leather shoes, was medium height and a bit on the big side. As Gigi walked past me, I caught a whiff of a flowery scent. She sported glasses and was dressed in a black pencil skirt with a silk red top. She was slightly taller and bigger than Jimmy. Gigi carried her weight well, like a sumptuous huge diamond ring. During that time in Zimbabwe, a voluptuous woman denoted wealth and good health. It was like the new IPhone, everyone wants one. She appeared like she was in a hurry to leave. Before leaving she invited us to her house for dinner that Saturday night.

After they left Dracul explained that they had two dwellings, one for the kids and one for them with Gigi's little girl. I pondered over their living arrangement. How strange it was to me that the children had one residence while they had another.

Saturday night Gigi picked me up. Dracul had spent the day with Jimmy at the shop and was going to meet us at the house for dinner at 7:30pm. On the way, Gigi talked about how her business kept her busy, and how she did not have time to hang out with friends. After 15 minutes of driving she announced, "We are here".

The headlights allowed for full visibility as the car stopped in front of a huge double black iron gate. She pressed the intercom button.

"Hello who is this?" A woman's voice asked.

"It's me Sandra open the gate please," said Gigi.

"Yes ma'am," her voice pierced through the intercom.

In the center of each gate there was a large gold letter 'G'. The gate opened slowly and Gigi drove slowly up the long, uphill driveway guided by the lights strung under the long line of trees flanking the drive. As we drove towards the house, I was taken by how large it was. Rooted in the attractiveness of the hill, stood a two-story brown brick residence built on the top of a mountain. A massive house, the kind every Zimbabwean kid dreamt of growing up.

Gigi parked outside the garage where a man and a woman were waiting. "Get all the bags in the trunk, lock the car and bring my keys," she barked.

"Certainly ma'am," the short stout man said.

Shaking my hand gently the woman and man greeted me. Gigi turned towards me, "Sylvia meet Betty and David; they are a couple and both work for me," Gigi boosted. "This is Dracul's girlfriend visiting from Harare," she added.

Betty wore a fitted pink dress with buttons up front with a black cap and apron. David donned black overalls and wellington boots.

Gigi signaled me to follow her. We entered the house into a spacious kitchen with an enormous granite island. The scent of onions and garlic lingered the air causing my mouth to water. We stopped as the cook extended her greetings. As soon as she opened her mouth I recognized the voice; it was the same voice that came through the intercom.

"Sandra this is Sylvia, and Sylvia this is Sandra my chef. She cooks delicious meals," Gigi said.

I stood there while Gigi gave instructions to Sandra, hoping she did not notice me scanning the kitchen. I could not help but notice the stainless-steel appliances which were complemented by the pendant lighting above the island. Gigi asked me to follow her again. I walked out of the kitchen and noticed glass front cabinets on either side of the far wall. It became apparent to me that Gigi was comfortable.

I stepped into the living room on an oatmeal colored furry floor. Gigi motioned me to sit on a tan leather chair next to a large wooden display cabinet with pictures and ornaments. Betty walked in with a glass of Coca-Cola setting it on the railway sleeper glass topped coffee table surrounded by two couches and a chair I was sitting on. Gigi excused herself and I took the liberty to examine my surroundings. Sitting on a gigantic stone fireplace were two grand china vases. There were massive windows dressed with orange and burgundy drapery panels coordinating with the cushions on the chairs. The room was beautiful in its opulence.

The men arrived joining Gigi and me in the living room. The smell of cigarettes on their clothing diluted the lovely scent of fresh flowers. Jimmy and Dracul talked about politics and football while consuming various alcoholic beverages. They indulged first in beer then wine, moved on to whisky and finally brandy. While they imbibed, Gigi sipped a glass of wine while telling me how she started her business at 25 and was now independent. A Cyndi Lauper played softly in the back ground.

We were interrupted by Sandra when she came in to let Gigi know that dinner was ready. "Alright people, dinner is ready now. Follow me to the dining room," Gigi announced.

As I followed her through the double doors into the dining-room, I noticed a vintage chandelier hanging from the ceiling above a mahogany table. There was cushy seating for eight people. The smell of roasted chicken wafting in the room ignited my appetite. Jimmy sat next to me opposite Gigi and I opposite Dracul. The sterling silver cutlery appeared as if it had been dried and buffed with a microfiber cloth, making me look upside down as I noticed my reflection on the silver spoon. There were two enormous paintings of the President and First Lady of Zimbabwe hanging side by side on the wall.

We were interrupted by a loud buzzing sound from the hallway. It was the phone. Startled, Jimmy jumped then excused himself to get the call. After about five minutes he returned to the table and Gigi quickly asked, "Who was that?"

I was so hungry at that point I was tempted to pick up my fork and start flexing it, waiting for the meal to start.

"That was Luke's mom. (One of his ex-wives) She stopped by the house and she thinks Luke is ill," he said still standing in a stooped posture with one hand resting on the chair.

"Well dinner is getting cold. We have been waiting for you. Have a seat and eat will you," she said dismissing Jimmy's obvious concern for his son.

The sound of the deep breaths he took were so loud, I'm sure they could be heard a mile away. I cut my eyes at Dracul; he picked up his bottle of lager and took a long sip.

Jimmy shook his head slowly. I noticed his Adam's apple moving up and down as he swallowed hard followed by his mouth falling open.

"Luke is a very sick kid. I need to go check on him. I will not enjoy dinner not knowing," said Jimmy.

I crossed my arms as I shifted in my chair, and noticed that Dracul was doing the same in his chair.

With her eyes wide open, lifting a single eyebrow Gigi said, "You can go after dinner. His mother can take care of the situation."

"I have to go, it sounded serious. You guys eat without me. I will be back soon," he said walking out of the dining room. I glanced at Dracul and showing his palm he shrugged. I looked down at the table rubbing my forehead. Dracul and I continued to sit quietly as we gave each other quick looks.

"Jimmy, are you kidding me? Come back here now."

"I got to go, see you soon. This is my baby we are talking about."

"In that case, take your brother and his girlfriend with you. No one is going to eat dinner."

"Come on guys, we have to go," screamed Jimmy looking at us on his way out.

Dracul motioned me to come with him. I took my jacket and followed Dracul through the kitchen and outside to the driveway, where Jimmy was already sitting on the driver's side with the engine running.

As he drove to his house, he poured out how Gigi was not reasonable. We just listened. On arrival, his three-year-old son, Luke, had fever and was throwing up profusely. Jimmy told us to stay home while he and Luke's mother took him to the emergency room. Before leaving the house, Jimmy instructed the maid to prepare something to eat. Fortunately, there was some leftover food. After dinner, I retired to bed.

The following morning, I was surprised to see Jimmy coming out of his bedroom. He stayed for the night at the children's house. He went to the shop and returned about lunch time to collect Dracul and me because he wanted us to visit his shop. After hanging out at his shop he decided to take us to one of Gigi's shops.

When we arrived, Gigi's car was parked in front and he commented that she was there. She was talking to a customer when we walked in, and she ignored Jimmy when he said hello. I quickly glanced at Jimmy then looked away. She greeted Dracul and me and offered us drinks. Jimmy turned to Dracul and suggested we leave since she was not talking to him. He drove us to his house, and then returned to his shop.

That evening, we were sitting in the living room and Mukadota, a famous Zimbabwean comedian, was on the television when Gigi showed up. She told Dracul and me that she really wanted us to have dinner at her house if we could come with her. Dracul told her only if Jimmy was coming would we come. "He can only come if he does not leave the table before we finish dinner," she sulked.

During dinner Jimmy was trying to explain the difference between the two bottles of wine on the table, and Gigi corrected him twice. I noticed him hunch down further and cringe as she continued to correct him. After dinner, he asked me to dance with him. We danced to 'Time after Time', by Cyndi Lauper. He chatted with me as we danced, reminding me that I was marrying into a good family. I wondered if that was what married life all about. Their relationship left me with unanswered questions.

Vee and I returned to Harare the following day.

Chapter 7: Bride Price

In the Shona culture, to which I belong, roora (bride price) is aimed at bringing the two families together. It shows that the bride is valuable in the marriage and above all, the groom's capability of taking care of the bride and future children. Roora takes place in several stages and each stage has its own traditions and small amounts to pay.

My father was tough to convince getting married at eighteen years old was ok. Without his approval, the marriage was not going to happen. I had just finished 'O' Levels (equivalent to 12th grade in the USA) and was in the middle of deciding whether to go into nursing or accounting as a profession. My father was so disappointed with me at that time because the marriage was not by choice, but because I was pregnant.

It was suggested that the only person who could convince my father otherwise was his mother, my grandmother. My grandmother lived in the village and I had to go get her. Growing up, I visited my grandmother every year during the four-week school holiday. I used to look forward to going to the village to hanging out with my cousins.

We would go to the fields, cow gatherings, and walk about six miles every Sunday to go to church at the Holy Cross Mission with my grandmother. This time it was different. The reason for my visit was somewhat complicated. I had to break the news to my grandmother that I was expecting, getting married and that I needed her to talk to my father to convince him to agree. Further, I had never been to our village in Masvingo on my own and now it seemed intimidating.

I arrived at my grandmother's and we spent a pleasant evening talking. I did not broach the reason for my visit. The following morning, as we walked to the river to take a bath, I decided to break the news.

"Grandmother my boyfriend and I would like to get married and father is not exactly thrilled. Would you come to Harare with me and talk to father for me please?"

"Getting married?" she asked.

Grandmother did not say a word until we started bathing. She stared at my naked body with squinted narrowed eyes. It didn't take long for her to confront me.

"Why are you rushing to get married, are you pregnant?" she asked.

"Not at all," I lied. "My boyfriend and I are madly in love."

I was scared that if she found out I was pregnant, she might refuse to return with me to convince my father.

I was astounded when grandmother agreed to come with me. I was even more astonished when she suggested that we catch the first bus the next day.

Grandmother had suggested we sleep in her mud hut kitchen with a thatched roof, because it was warmer. There was always an open fire burning to cook food being made from scratch. I woke up at dawn to the warmth and smell of wood smoke that circulated through the kitchen like a burning lavender candle. Granny had put more wood into the fire illuminating the hut so I could see while I got ready for our rather long walk to the bus stop. It was about 10km (6.2 miles) away. I had walked that 10 km only couple of days ago. I spotted the bus from afar and let out a huge breath.

My trip paid off. My father agreed to accept bride price and the date for the ceremony was set for the end of spring. As spring ended, bride price date was agreed. The big day was on a Saturday afternoon and the weather was on our side. The house was full of joyous people. It felt like it was back in 1980 when it was announced that ZANU PF had won and Zimbabwe had gained its independence. I was only thirteen but I remember the excitement in the whole country, on the bus, shops, schools, clinics, churches everywhere. Little did we know that it was the start of the downfall of our country. Perhaps that should have been a sign for me. In a decade, most Zimbabweans myself included, would leave our motherland in search of greener pastures in the western world.

I woke and suddenly it hit me that my boyfriend was coming to pay the bride price that day. I looked on the opposite side of the room where my half-sister and little sister, whom I shared a bedroom with, were dead to the world. I glanced at the clock on the wall and it was striking five o'clock. *Too early to get out of bed*, I thought. I lay there imagining what was ahead of me.

Not able to sleep, I decided to try my new dress that I was to wear that day to impress Dracul and his family. I contemplated the effects in the full-length mirror on the wardrobe door. The dress was a knee-length floral dress that showed my slim body. I was disappointed at the idea of wearing a wraparound cloth over it, a sign to show respect to Dracul's family.

I heard the clanking of dishes followed by my aunt's high pitched voice, "Good morning mom, did you sleep well?" she asked my grandmother. I knew it was time to get up. I woke my sisters and we went into the kitchen.

"Okay young ladies, today is your big day, the house needs to be spotless and we need to do some cooking," said aunt.

The kitchen filled with a quick ripping sizzle sound when meat was put into the pan. The aroma of the browning meat filled the kitchen and could be smelled as one entered the front gate. Under my aunt's directions, my cousins, sisters, and I, were busy cooking for our guests.

Excitement was in the air. Everyone had to be presentable including children. The house had to spotless to impress the groom and his family. First impressions were vital to the perception of the groom's family about the bride's family. Thomas Mapfumo was playing in the background in the living room, while waiting for the ceremony to commence.

It was finally time to get ready. I tried to hold in every emotion that was building inside of me. It was a mix of excitement and fear. It was my dowry day and I wanted to make a good impression. "Do I look okay?" I kept asking my cousins and sisters. I checked my appearances in the mirror one more time before stepping out of the girl's room.

By noon, the living room was filled with adult relatives including my mother. This was my mother's first time returning to the house since divorcing my father.

"I would not miss this day for anything," she told me. Mom brought her two sisters with her for support.

As the eldest girl, this was my family's first experience in marital process. I sat at the kitchen table with my cousins and sisters and made sure the door was slightly propped open so we could hear what was being said in the living room. We heard a knock on the front door; my sister peeped through the crack of the door.

"Munyayi is here," she whispered.

My stomach churned and I felt my chest tightening. This was the first stage of the process. Munyayi, a go-between came to my house to inform my family of Dracul's intentions of marrying me. I was asked to come into the living room briefly just to confirm that I knew these people, then I was summoned back to the kitchen. In the meantime, Dracul and his family members waited at Aunt Rhoda's house.

My confirming meant that Dracul and his family were welcomed to come to my house. When they arrived, they were welcomed with loud cheers (mhururu) from women relatives then ushered into a separate room. Sneaking a glance over my shoulder into the groom's room, I saw Dracul sitting on the floor in the corner of the room rubbing the back of his neck.

The Lobola negotiations were the first official meeting of our families. For me, bride price isn't about the money but about knowing and getting acquainted with each other. It's not about selling your daughter or buying a daughter-in-law as some people believe.

Before the ceremony Munyayi was given a list of groceries to give to Dracul to bring to my family. Dracul had to bring the exact items and quantities on the list as a sign of respect towards my family. The list included 10kg bags of rice, potatoes, cooking oil, vegetables, beans, maize meal, sacks of onions, meat, crates of beer and bottled soft drinks.

The next step was for my family to ask for a 'ndiro' (plate) from Munyayi. With the plate placed in the center of the floor, a process called 'vhuramuromo' (meaning opening of mouth), where Dracul had to place a small fee in order for my family to start talking. I wanted to be in the same room as everyone else, however traditionally I was not needed. I sat in the kitchen listening very hard so as not to miss anything. I began to feel that it was not fair that this was all about me and I was not allowed to be in the room. My thoughts were interrupted by an abrupt sharp sound (special traditional greeting) 'Gusvi', as Munyayi announced his arrival. My sisters, cousins and I listened to each stage of the ceremony in absolute silence. Only our light breathing could be heard.

Zvireverere Zvababa (Gifts for the father) was the next stage. The main payment for my father was

'Matekenyandebvu'. This was to acknowledge him for "the pulling of his beard" as I sat on his knee and putting up with my playful antics as a child.

My mother gifts came next. Her payments were for 'mbereko', for carrying me in her womb for nine months and on her back as a child. Mom had discussed the price she would ask with her sisters prior to the ceremony. The $700 price was not negotiable.

Mbudzi yedare Goat, (yemachinda), another part of the ceremony, Dracul was supposed to bring a live goat to be slaughtered during the payment process. The goat was supposed to be cooked and served after the ceremony. Because we were in the city and could not slaughter and cook the goat, Dracul paid a fee that was shared among all my brothers.

I participated twice during the process; confirming that I knew the people and the second time when I was asked to pick money from the plate for myself. The money was to go towards the purchase of household goods or cooking utensils. I recall hesitating to take the money and my aunt had to nudge me as if to ask 'what are you waiting for'? I don't remember how much I picked-up.

The negotiations part of the ceremony occurred the following day. The next vital stage was the Rusambo (Dowry). This stage was only reached after the above stages had been fulfilled. Rusambo is the bigger portion of the bride price. As I listened to the amount that was charged, I scratched my jaw shaking my head. I looked at my cousin and her eyes were wide open. I'm not quite sure how I felt—it was overwhelming and way more than I could comprehend at the time.

The next stage Danga (Livestock), equally important as Rusambo, was to be reached only after 'Rusambo'. Since I was getting married in the city, my father did not expect Dracul's family to bring a herd of cattle with him, instead he asked for the equivalent sum of money from Dracul.

My understanding is that it is usually between seven to eight cows and one of them is for the mother and is known as "mombe yeumai'. If the woman has a child out of wedlock, you might knock off a cow or two. Luckily for my father I was only eighteen and pregnant, so he charged extra money called 'damage', for impregnating me before paying roora. Most young men didn't have eight cows at their disposal so the payment of cows could be paid in installments, and that was the agreement.

I wondered why father did not charge for more cows. To my horror Munyayi started bargaining with father for six cows instead of the eight that father was charging. It sounded like they were bargaining for a clothing item on a reduced-price rack with an additional ten percent discount with a voucher.

Raising his voice father said, "Take it or leave it. It is eight cows or nothing. I cannot believe I am negotiating my 18-year-old daughter's bride price. I should be discussing her career," he added.

At that moment, I realized how seriously disappointed my father was with me. I couldn't fill my lungs completely. I thought, *'here we go, he is going to change his mind last minute'.*

My mom's cow was very important because this was to acknowledge the spiritual symbolism, so hers was taken care of no matter what. The discussions about the cash equivalent for the livestock my father had asked for was very gentle, humble and respectful in the end. Dracul paid the price of 8 cows.

The final stage was the gift of clothes that Dracul was expected to buy for my father and mother. Dracul and his family were allowed to join my family in the other room, a sign of being accepted into the family as a son-in-law. Suddenly I heard a sharp sound as he greeted my parents with a special traditional greeting 'Gusvi.' At this point he was given a list of clothing that both my father and mother chose. I recall it was full attire from top to bottom.

It was time for the two families to mix and mingle as well as eat and drink. Chibuku (traditional beer), was passed around as men patiently waited their turn to sip. Men both old and young (especially groom's side), sat on the floor, a sign of respect, as they took generous sips.

~~~

A week after the ceremony, I decided to go meet the rest of Dracul's family in the village. My sister Evelyn escorted me. Traditionally, I had to be covered in white from head to toe so that no one could see me. As I walked into the village, Dracul's family started dancing and howling. My sister and I took our time walking while the whole village teased us and encouraged us to keep walking. They threw money at my feet and they sang songs about how happy they were. Eventually I was escorted into my future mother in law's home where I was encouraged to take off my veil with gifts and pleadings. That is when the rest of the family got to see me for the first time.

CHAPTER 8: The First Wedding

My sister and I returned to the city after a few days and I moved in with Dracul. Within eight weeks after the bride price ceremony, it was time to prepare for my white wedding; so I thought. To my dismay, Dracul told me that Gigi was making all the arrangements including picking my wedding dress. *"How does she know what I like or my size?"* I thought to myself. I was instructed to pick six bridesmaids and to participate in the bridal team dance (wedding dance steps).

I hired a wedding dance choreographer who lived down the street to teach the team wedding dance routines. The songs were picked by the choreographer in advance and used during practice. The dance is similar to American line dancing. It is a choreographed dance with a repeated sequence of steps in which the bridal team dance in two lines facing the same directions or sometimes facing each other.

The wedding was taking place at Dracul's family's rural home. The homestead consisted of a group of thatch-roofed (rondavels) arranged in a circular way leaving a big open space in the middle. Among the huts was a kitchen, barns, store houses, as well as a brick house with some rooms and a living room. A few meters away from the huts there were men's and women's pit toilets and there was no electricity.

The morning of my wedding, as I lie there looking at the sunrise through the window wondering what my wedding dress was going to look like, there was a knock on the door. I shared one of the rooms in the brick house with my bridesmaids. My maid of honor, Jennifer, answered the door, and all of us gasped. Gigi stood right before us carrying a wedding gown bag.

"Can I come in?" she asked.

"Sure", I responded with a slow smile.

"Here, try your dress. You are going to love it," she bragged.

Gigi had arrived from Bulawayo in the early hours of the morning. Among my wedding dress, she had also brought bridesmaids dresses which she got her friend to make and most of the groceries for the wedding including the cake. Tilting my head to the side with raised eyebrows, I reached for the dress. As I took the dress out of the gown bag, I picked it up and it had something unsettling about its smell. I looked at Jennifer to make certain that she sensed the smell too. It smelled like a sour smell of stomach churning.

The dress was ivory lace with long sleeves and came with a pair of lace fingerless gloves with ruffle and a pillbox hat with the veil. The lace looked like plastic and it was all over the dress. I put the dress over my head to put it on. I felt like I was going to be sick as the smell swiftly travelled up my nostrils causing me to gag.

"Are you alright, Sylvia?" Jennifer asked.

"I am fine I need to sit down," I said.

Because I was eight months pregnant, the girls thought it was due to the pregnancy. I had been worried for months about how (and if) it would fit; the dress was slightly big. The gloves looked like mittens when I put them on.

Around noon, as I advanced out of the house making my way to the ceremony, the curling clouds of smoke from the kitchen and the big fire outside where the African beer had been prepared for days filled the air, and the happy screams of guests, families and friends walking to the church could be heard in a distance.

Below a golden glow that spread across the sky as the sun chased the dark clouds, stood uncountable fruit trees surrounding the green church where the wedding ceremony took place.

Stepping out of the blue Peugeot owned by Jimmy, among the crowd in front of the church, I spotted Dracul immediately, dressed in a grey suit as were all the groomsmen.

As for me, I felt that if anything, my wedding dress had added ten years to me. The difference between my eighteen years and his twenty-six had vanished; not as obvious as it was that morning. Above all, I did not feel elegant or beautiful. Even on supposedly 'the best day of my life' I could not convince myself of that. I knew that my dress was oversized and fingerless gloves on my hands looked like a newborn's mittens.

Jennifer had done my hair that morning. She put all her strength and passion into straightening and curling my hair only to be flattened by placing the pillbox wedding hat right on top of my head. Gigi insisted I wear it because it was part of the wedding dress. The bridesmaid dresses were homemade. Looking around me, I decided that my dress was absolutely not a contender. My bridesmaids looked better dressed than I.

I could hear the church choir crescendo from the open door as we drew closer. I accepted my father's arm by resting my gloved hand on it. The crowd cheered and danced as we walked into the church.

The main entry was arched and the doors leading from the vestibule into the church had a double wooden door with crosses on either side. I noticed a large crucifix behind the altar on the back wall. On both sides of the side walls there were a few arched windows with concrete lintels that bond them with the arched entry. I walked down the main isle of the church carrying my bridal bouquet of roses, tulips and daisies in my left and my right laced through the arm of my escort. The floors were concrete and the clacking sound my shoes made as we walked towards the pulpit, made me feel self-conscious especially since all eyes were on the bride - me. The priest stood in the alter

waiting for us to take our seats.

I was filled with mixed emotions as my father

walked me down the aisle. Part of me was happy that I was

escaping Judith's abuse, at the same time I was worried for

my siblings, particularly Prosper who was just 10 years old.

Although my father was putting on a happy face, I knew

this is not what he wanted for me. Instead of being happy

and all smiles for a day that was supposed to be the best

day of my life, I was worried sick. Being 8 months

pregnant didn't help either. I had no choice this was my

wedding day; I was getting married. Then there was the

culture belief that brides shouldn't express their emotions

freely especially on your wedding day, you don't want to

be over zealous. It might give the groom's family

impression that you not reserved. Being seen as reserved

was more desirable than being loud and drawing attention.

A fly would land on my mouth and I would completely

ignore it, like Senator Hillary Clinton during the debate with Trump.

The reception took place in the big open space surrounded by huts. Rhythm and clothing are important aspects of the Zimbabwean bridal dance team. Bridesmaids wore matching dresses and shoes. The bridegrooms wore matching suits. The entrance bridal party dance rejuvenated the guests at the wedding. As they danced to the fast entrance song, a cloud of dust rose around them almost to their knees.

Slowly the warm golden glow stretched over the fields behind us. Gigi ordered me to go change into a maternity dress she bought for me before cutting the cake. I could not wait to get out of the wedding dress, pillbox hat and the mittens. It was a below knee length, long sleeved floral maternity dress. The sleeves were too long. I had to roll them up twice before doing the buttons up.

"I will take this dress anytime instead of the wedding gear," I whispered in Jennifer's ear and she giggled.

A few hours after cutting the wedding cake, Gigi approached me and told me that if I was tired I could be excused. Jennifer and I seized the opportunity to get away and dashed to our room. As we lay there reflecting on the events of the day, I heard Jennifer snoring and I blew the candle out and fell asleep.

CHAPTER 9: Married Life

Back in Harare, a week after our wedding, we spent our honeymoon in Eastlea one of compact Harare suburbs, preparing for the birth of our son. Contained inside a zinc-coated chain linked fence with a two-way lockable gate, was a sky blue one story fairly-sized house that we shared with Dracul's brother-in-law, Herbert.

It was in late February 1987 my son was five months old. I had been married for six months. From the bedroom, I smelled a sewage drain odor lingering in the air. Suddenly I recognized the smell because one of my brothers had smoked marijuana with his friends and got into big trouble with father.

It was kind like mistaking Wasabi for guacamole as the smell whizzed up my nostrils filling up my lungs compromising by breathing. I put the baby in the crib and followed the smell to the bathroom. I grabbed the wooden bathroom door handle but the door was locked. I knocked on the wooden bathroom door which had some of its white paint peeling off.

I knew Dracul was in there. "Open the door please I need to pee," I lied.

"Hold on." After about a minute, he opened the door and the smell created a choking sensation in my throat.

"Are you smoking marijuana?

"No, I am not."

"Come on, I can smell it."

With my arms folded over my stomach, I asked, "So how long have you been smoking marijuana?"

"I am dependent on it," Dracul said. "I have been dreading this conversation. I promise to get help if you do not tell your family, particularly Evelyn," he added as he walked out of the bathroom.

It reminded me of an African Proverb-Marriage is like a groundnut, you have to crack it to see what is inside-Ghanaian Proverb.

For most of my life I had always thought of Marijuana as this deadly, life robbing drug that takes people's lives, in fact I viewed it on the same level as crack or cocaine today. Every time I imagined Dracul smoking, it felt like my heart was shrinking.

The Beatings

My little sister Elizabeth started visiting me on weekends. One Saturday as we sat at the kitchen table she said, "Those jeans look really good on you."

"Thanks," Dracul said.

Dracul's figure was almost perfect then. At that time, it did not occur to me that she had a crush on her brother-in-law.

Customarily it is okay for a brother-in-law to flirt with his sister-in-law. Watching my husband flirting with my little sister made me feel disgusted and angry. He acted incredibly inappropriate around my sister. I knew it was not right for him to fondle her breast, but to my surprise my sister appeared comfortable with it. At first, I did not want to believe it. My sister Evelyn's husband had tried to flirt with me in the past; I made it clear I was not interested. I thought my sister was sweet and quiet, falling for my husband was the last thing I could have seen coming.

That evening the three of us watched television in the living room. I left briefly to go check on my baby. Returning, I noticed that Dracul had moved next to her. I also noticed that he was jumpy when I walked into the room as if he had been caught at something he obviously shouldn't have been doing. My stomach quivered as I cleared my throat. I sat between Dracul and my sister on the brown leather couch.

A few hours later, returning to the room again, I caught a glimpse of him stroking my sister's breast. A flush of adrenaline rushed through my body. Pulling my sister from the couch, I turned to Dracul and said, "You are disgusting."

"You are getting paranoid for no reason," he commented.

I assumed the worst-case scenario-my husband was sleeping with my blood sister. I confided in my big sister Evelyn.

"She would never do that. You are just paranoid," she said dismissing me.

The following weekend, before midnight on a Friday, my husband got home smelling like happy hour, accompanied by Elizabeth. This surprised me because I had not invited her. I felt inside me that something was going on between my husband and sister. I sent her to bed in the guest bedroom.

"Where are you coming from at this hour with my sister?"

"I thought you would need help with housework this weekend and taking care of the baby," he reasoned.

I tossed and turned with my eyes wide open for hours, unable to sleep. Around 4am, pretending like I was fast asleep, I observed my husband sneaking out of our bedroom. My heart pounded as if it was going to burst through my chest. I got up and followed him trying to be as quiet as I could. He made his way to my sister's room. At that juncture, my adrenaline shot up like an enormous kite caught by the wind.

"Where the hell do you think you are going?" I shouted.

"I thought this was the bathroom. I must have gotten disoriented because I have been drinking," he responded, startled by my presence.

"Nonsense," I said. "You brought my sister here at midnight without my permission. Now you are trying to sneak in her bed," I screamed.

"You are out of your mind. I can have any woman I want. I do not want anything from a 15-year-old," he said defending himself.

In the morning, I gave my sister taxi fare and ordered her to leave immediately. I reminded her that she could only visit when I invited her. I went to Evelyn's that afternoon. I could hear and feel the breaks in my voice as I told her what had transpired the previous night. For the first time, she took me seriously.

I did not see Elizabeth for about a month. I visited my dad and Elizabeth expressed that she missed me and nothing was going on between my husband and her. I wanted to believe her although my sixth sense was fighting me, telling me she was lying. I ignored my sixth sense.

That afternoon we went to the city together. Around lunch time, as we strolled on First Street doing window shopping, we ran into my high school sweetheart, Mark. He offered to buy us lunch which I accepted. After lunch my sister and I parted ways. I returned home and she went back to my dad's.

One nippy June evening, four weeks after running into Mark, thoughts about what to cook the next day for my visitors were interrupted when Dracul asked me "If you were to meet your ex-boyfriend in the city what would you do?"

His question seemed to have come out of nowhere. It did not occur to me that Elizabeth could have spied on me.

Suddenly my jaws locked. I could not believe what he had just asked me. Choosing my words carefully, so I thought, "I would ignore him totally."

"Liar!" he screamed.

I noticed his eyes were completely enraged. I tried to get out of his way but as I stood, his open palm found my face. Stunned that he hit me, my face stinging, I could not move. The beating continued. He punched me, closed fist, repeatedly in the face. With each punch, I would fall to the ground and struggle to get up again. I staggered trying again to get away but he grabbed me by my braids. It was horribly painful and I screamed. He let go then.

I was able to get up and went to the kitchen looking for a weapon. I picked up one of the saucepans and came back into the bedroom. I aimed the pan at him but it missed him knocking the Zimbabwe Bird carving on the dressing table. I looked around the room to see if I could find something else. I grabbed the carving, and he jumped on me twisting my right arm causing me to let go the carving. He pinned me down for a few minutes to calm me down.

The following day he bought me red roses and an 'I am sorry card' where he wrote, "I lost my temper and I know I was wrong for it. I don't want to repeat this ever again." He signed it 'I love you'. I believed his apology.

On another occasion, about 3pm in the afternoon on a Wednesday, I was getting ready to do some ironing and decided to step outside to get laundry that was drying on the line. As the door slammed behind me, I realized I had just locked myself out.

The door had a deadbolt lock that required the key to open from the outside. I panicked because my toddler son was inside and I had beef cooking on the stove. I felt feverish by the panic and began grabbing at my hair at the same time. I paced up and down the back garden then remembered that the bedroom window was open. The window was long; below my knee height but had windows bars to deter thieves. Cracking my neck from side to side, I mustered all my strength and kicked at the bars a few times, hoping to kick them off the window frame. Unfortunately, I was not strong enough.

I started smelling the beef and I knew that the beef had started burning. *"My baby, I need to get to him before the house is covered in smoke."* I was sweating buckets. I began calling his name. Following my voice, he crawled into the bedroom and to the window. Reaching out, I grabbed his arm and pulled him to the window. Although I couldn't get him out, I knew that he would get some fresh air at least.

Within minutes I could smell the burning beef, and saw smoke in the kitchen. *"Dang why didn't I take the keys or my baby with me? Dracul should be home in an hour,"* I thought. I prayed that he came home straightaway.

I stood still by the window holding on to my baby. I felt like throwing up from the pain building in the back of my throat. After an hour and a half Dracul finally arrived. By that time the whole house was covered in smoke including the bedroom.

"Get inside and get the baby." I said hurriedly.

I went back in the house and the smoke was unbelievable.

"So explain again what happened?" demanded Dracul.

"I forgot the keys and locked myself out." I said.

"You are brainless. You should know by now that you have to take the keys with you every time you go outside." He screamed.

Before I could respond, he slapped me across the face

and kicked me in the stomach. With my head tilted to one side,

I said, "I saved our son's life, I stood with him by the window for

more than an hour so he didn't suffocate."

"Shut up!" he shouted. "Nonsense; you are the most

stupid woman I have ever met. Consider yourself lucky to be

married to someone like me. I have to go for a drink to stand

you," he finished, walking out of the house.

I felt my world tilting once again. I sat down reflecting

rubbing the middle of my forehead. I thought he was going to

be proud of me for thinking fast and saving our son's life, but he

didn't want to acknowledge that. For days after this incident I

was quieter and less animated.

~~~~

To my surprise in April 1987, Dracul suggested I go

back to school and take English language classes. I needed

a grade better than C to be accepted in college. The only

option for me was to take night classes at a local school while he took care of the baby.

One night in the middle of June 1987 I was walking from school, and I noticed a person behind a tree. I started running towards home. When I got home Dracul was not there, and then he showed up after a few minutes. Still trembling I told him about the person who was hiding behind a tree and casually he said, "Be careful."

It was a chilly Tuesday evening, two weeks after the school incident when again I noticed a figure behind a tree. However, this time I recognized the person, it was Dracul. I covered my mouth and nose with the collar of my jacket, as I confronted him, "Why are you spying on me?"

"You told me you were sacred so I came to pick you up," he answered quickly,

The last Friday in November 1987, Dracul invited me to his end of year office party. I requested time to think about it. The beatings had become a routine. Being in public places with Dracul was a recipe for disaster.

"If you are not interested let me know. I will need time to find someone to take with me," he mumbled walking out of the kitchen. "I give you a couple of hours," he shouted from the back garden while smoking marijuana.

Standing at the kitchen sink looking out the window, I weighed the pros and cons. I became quiet and my body felt heavy. I kept myself busy tidying up around the kitchen waiting for the hours to be up. Less than twenty minutes into the two hours he gave me, he entered the kitchen filling the air with the burnt odor of his pot.

"I need an answer now," he screamed.

I reluctantly I accepted the invitation.

The following evening, after dropping our son at my cousin, we headed to a local hotel in the city where the end of year office party was being held. We strolled into this fancy lobby where everyone looked elegant in their formal wear. I felt like I belonged in my small satin knee length black dress. I had never attended a year end office party before. Soft rock music echoed in the background as people mingled. There was a table of appetizers and an open bar with a bartender.

"I am going get to us drinks," said Dracul vanishing into the crowd.

I found myself abandoned and feeling awkward. Staring down at my feet, I stood there in the middle of the lobby waiting for him to return. After sometime he returned with our drinks and he handed me mine. I took a sip out of courtesy. The drink tasted of beetroot; certainly not one I would have chosen for myself.

Dracul started walking towards a couple standing near the entrance and I followed.

"Hello Mr. and Mrs. Jones," Dracul said shaking both their hands. "Meet my wife, Sylvia."

Mr. Jones extended a thin hand with long bony fingers and gave me a gentle squeeze. He was elegantly dressed in a double breasted brown suit, tailored to fit his tall slim figure like a glove. His wife stood 5.9 and was also beautifully dressed draped in a long floral gown with a slit up the side a mile long. The dress was complemented with dazzling gold earrings and a thick chain. "Who is watching the little one?" asked Mrs. Jones. Before I responded Dracul said, "Our cousin is babysitting."

After the introduction, Dracul led the way into the ballroom. The carpet was thick beneath my feet and was heavily patterned. In the middle of the room hung an enormous crystal chandelier emitting light so bright, I was blinded for a moment as I gazed at it.

"We will sit here," he said pointing at a vacant table next to the dance floor. By now I had learned that the only thing Dracul and I had in common was our passion for music and dancing. The wooden dance floor was big enough to fit twenty jive dancers. The room had more than 10 tables able to seat 8. Satin red tablecloths reflected the lights and were set with gold hand-painted plates set atop chargers. There were two bottles of wine at each table.

The Chief Executive Officer (CEO) introduced himself as Mr. Jones and I recognized him straight away. Soon after a couple of speeches from two senior guys, it was time for dinner. The tantalizing aroma of grilled beef ribs was in the air as the table next to us was served. It was not long before we were served the scrumptious meal of barbequed ribs. They were cooked to perfection-charred, crusty, falling off the bone, crispy on the outside and juicy on the inside.

After the meal, we hit the dance floor, dancing to a few Michael Jackson songs, Thomas Mapfumo and Bob Marley. Dracul dismissed himself going outside to smoke. When he returned, I was sitting at the table talking to one of his co-workers. I thought he was going to join us. Instead he walked to the dance floor. I joined him but he ignored me. I wondered what I had done wrong.

"Follow me," he demanded.

My shoulders tightened as I trailed behind him, my feet rustling in the carpet, to the parking lot.

"What were you talking about with my co-worker?"

"He was asking about the baby and what I do for a living, that's all," I hesitated. Looking around the parking lot, he put his cigarette out on my right cheek. I stood rooted to the ground despite the burning pain in the center of my cheek. He sprinted towards the car. I took my heels off and took after him but before I realized what was happening, he jumped into the car and drove off. I gasped, and my chest tingled. Tears welled in my eyes. I knew what was coming. I had suffered beatings from similar situations before.

After a few minutes, I decided to ask the CEO, Mr. Jones for a ride home. He appeared to be a respectable man and his wife was present. Fortunately for me as I walked back into the ballroom, Mr. Jones and his wife were leaving. I told them there was a misunderstanding and Dracul had left. On the way, I avoided going into details of what happened. Sensing that I did not want to talk about what had occurred, the Jones' talked about casual things during the drive to Eastlea. When we arrived, Mr. Jones gave me his business card and told me to call if I needed anything. I had them drop me off at my cousin's home because I was scared of what was waiting for me at home, 'a good beating'.

My cousin accompanied me home. Dracul was already in bed but when he looked at me it drove the monster inside him to the highest level of insanity. I wrapped my arms around my belly while I squeezed my eyes shut. My cousin had not left yet and in an effort to protect me, held Dracul in a bear hug as he charged at me. There was a smash as they landed on the bed breaking it in few places. My cousin did not leave that night and I was grateful she stayed `till crack of the dawn.

It wasn't long after my cousin left the beating began. Dracul punched me in the face repeatedly even as I begged him to stop. The beating seemed to be never ending this time. I was convinced that he was going to kill me this time but he stopped. My head felt like someone was banging it on a concrete wall as I curled my body into a ball on the couch. I had a black eye, cigarette burn, busted lip. I looked like I had been in a boxing match with Vinny Paz.

The very next afternoon he said, "If you had not spoken to that loser all this wouldn't have happened". He again promised that this would not happen again. But I'd heard that promise so many times before, I knew it was hollow. Dracul demanded I cooked him lunch so I did. I tried to eat but had no appetite. For the remainder of the day I wondered if this was what marriage was about. I hadn't signed up for this.

I had reached a point where I had no energy. My head felt like it was spinning all the time and walking on those eggshells was way more than I could do. There were times when the effects of the beatings even manifested as a sour taste in my mouth.

Over time, I began to feel like I had the flu 24/7 with the nausea, and sweating. Even my limbs began to feel heavy. When the tingling in my chest started, it made me wonder if I would have a heart attack even at my young age.

My sister's betrayal drove the feelings of hopelessness and loneliness even deeper. I had no self-esteem or worth. My despair began to take its toll on me. I pulled away from my friends including my best friend, Jennifer. I stopped knitting crocheting, reading, or even braiding my hair. And this was just when I was alone. In public, I felt humiliated, and wanted only to disappear—vanish into thin air.

Many times, I tried to hide the bruises and black eyes, or lie that I had tripped and fallen for fear of putting myself at greater risk of being beaten. I had nowhere to turn. There was no help but then I began to believe what people were saying—I deserved the beatings. I was blaming myself for everything.

His beatings were turning me into a quiet, scared, sad, pathetic, young teenage mother.

Chapter 10: The Cheating

It was winter 1988, 17 months into my marriage. Thembi, my cousin, told me she suspected that Dracul had been using her phone on weekends to talk to a woman he addressed as Doo.

"He always throws the torn paper with the telephone number in the trash when he is done," she told me.

My breathing got faster got faster as she told the story. It felt like I had been training for hours in boot camp. "Could you help me get the crumbled paper with the telephone number?" I asked.

That Saturday my husband told me he was going to work. He stopped at my cousin's to make a call to Doo. He had torn up the piece of paper with the telephone number written on it and threw it in the trash can as he routinely did. My cousin put it together and I had Doo's telephone number. I decided to call the number. A young boy answered the phone. I asked for Doo and he bluntly said the full name but, for the purpose of this book, I will continue calling her Doo, the little boy said Doo was not home.

I made up my mind that I would bring this to Dracul's attention. By this time, I had learned that when confronting Dracul about anything, I had to approach him with caution. I had memorized Doo's number, then a few days later I said to Dracul, "I have been having a dream about the same number for three days straight. I wonder if I should play the lottery or something.

"What is the number?" he asked.

"Here," I said handing him a piece of paper. He shifted in his chair while he stared at the piece of paper.

The following day, Dracul got very close to confessing. Sitting at the kitchen table, he told me that he was orienting a new girl at work by the name Doo.

"How is she doing"? I asked.

"So far so good", he responded.

I knew then that he knew I knew.

LOIS SCENE

In my culture the in-laws, that is the extended family members on both sides, has enormous influence on the marriage. Unfortunately, this influence can have negative impacts on marriages.

It was a Friday night at the end of April 1988 when Dracul busted into our bedroom as I sang my baby to sleep. He went straight to the cabinet where we kept cash.

"Where is my damn money?" he screamed waking the baby up.

"How much do you want?" I asked with a weak voice.

"All of it," he demanded. "I am taking my sister out."

My heart skipped a beat and I almost tripped over a pair of my house shoes as I walked to the other side of the room to get the cash.

Like Casper the friendly ghost, Lois, Dracul's big sister who was visiting from the village, appeared in the bedroom.

"Is she refusing to give you your money?" she asked Dracul to my horror. Turning towards me she ordered, "You do not work. It is not your money. Give my brother his money now."

Breathless and with a shaky hand, I handed all the money to Dracul.

I overhead her whispering to Dracul as they walked out of the room, "This woman needs a good beating. Who does she think she is?"

A few minutes later Dracul returned to the bedroom. I sat on the bed rocking my baby. "Next time when I ask for my money, you do not ask questions," he yelled.

My shoulders tightened and I felt like I was glued to the bed.

"I am talking to you woman," he screamed, punching me in the face.

To protect my child, I decided to put him in his crib, giving Dracul a good opportunity to punch and kick me. Lois came back to the room to rub it in.

"You deserve it. You think you own my brother? You are having a giggle."

"Please tell him to stop, he is hurting me," I begged Lois. I felt like I was trying to pee after an episiotomy. At that moment, Lois walked out of the room instead and the punches and blows continued.

After a period of time, I heard Lois from the other side of the door. "That is enough brother. Let us go now."

A couple of weeks went by and on a nippy Sunday evening coming from visiting my father, Dracul stopped at a gas station to pump some gas. While he was putting gas in the car, I opened the glove compartment and came across a photo of a lady and him kissing. It was painful, disrespectful and insulting. I felt my eyes watering and chin trembling. I took the photo and put it in my purse. All the way home my mind was racing thinking about what I was going to do with the photo. I had evidence he was cheating on me. There was no way he was going to deny it, I thought.

After the second or third beating, I had begun to be frightened of Dracul. I had stopped trying to defend myself physically or verbally but I was still not concerned enough to leave him. Most probably because I had come from a background were wife beating was common. Sometimes I wished I had my own voice but that desire was obscured by my fears of Dracul ending our marriage. I was scared to fend for myself, hurt my family and, above all, what people would say. At that time, I wasn't aware what this was doing to my confidence, self-esteem and my life.

Thankfully I had my sister. She was my best friend, and the only person in my life I felt I could share everything that was going on in my marriage. On Monday after Dracul left for work, I decided to tell Evelyn. With tears rolling down my cheeks, I handed her the photo.

"Enough is enough," she said, wiping the tears from my cheeks.

Evelyn came to my place later that evening. Dracul had just gotten home from work and was relaxing on the couch in the living room. Evelyn did not waste time. She stormed into the living, and threw the photo on his lap.

"Here explain this. You are always accusing my sister of cheating yet you are the one cheating." I followed Evelyn to the living room to hear what Dracul had to say for himself. He looked at me with an evil eye. I felt him squeezing my neck with his eyes.

Evelyn charged at Dracul before he responded and started punching, kicking and scratching him in the face with her long red finger nails. I noticed a little blood trickling from his right cheek. Dracul tried to get up but she threw herself on him. the couch made a cracking sound as they landed in a heap. He grabbed Evelyn's hands telling her to stop.

"Tell your stupid sister to stop this nonsense," he screamed at me. Holding my baby on my left hip, I stood there like a statue, thinking he had met his match.

At that moment, in my eyes, my sister was Wonder Woman. She was beating him up. What astonished me more was that he never tried to hit her back. Puffing and blowing, Evelyn carried on screaming, shouting and kicking her legs.

"Why are you doing this to my little sister?" she asked him.

"So you think you are her protector?" he said with an unmoved half smile.

My baby was so scared he began crying so I left the room.

After Evelyn left, I sat motionless for hours. I felt as if I have been soul sucked right out of me; I couldn't breathe. It felt like my vital organs had been yanked out of my body. I was scared stiff that Dracul was going to take it out on me, but surprisingly enough he did not.

Chapter 11: Retaliation

Infuriated by my sister's behavior, Dracul made sure I had no access to his money. He made all the purchases and when it came to food he provided only the main items that were needed to make Sadza, our staple food. Sadza is like rice, you can have it with any relish of your choice. My relish would become dried beans every day.

The beans were so dry, I had to eat them in the rain. My mouth ached and my throat was becoming raw. I was no longer allowed to speak to or visit my sister and could not leave the house unless I was with him. At the age of twenty, I was imprisoned in the house like Rapunzel in her tower. Time seemed to creep with the speed of a sloth. It was like being married to Lucifer.

In the days and weeks that followed, I felt my heart chipping slowly away in tiny pieces. My throat and lungs were sore as an abrasion on the palm of a hand and the world seemed to be in slow motion. One mid-morning Evelyn came to check on me. Luckily I was home alone. I had not seen her since her clash with Dracul over the photo. I broke the bad news to her that she was no longer allowed to visit me and vice versa.

"You don't need to live in captivity. Leave him. Come with me now. I will help you with your baby," Evelyn said with a shaky voice.

I could hear the pain in her voice. It was like I had just clamped her nipples with a battery clamp and left them there hanging while I went for a jog.

"He is just upset, let me give him time," I responded.

Sighing heavily, she collapsed onto a chair next to me. I still had hope. I had been disabled to the point of succumbing to his abuse.

My sister continued visiting at the times Dracul was at work. She would bring me chicken or beef stew so that I could have a break from dried beans. Afraid of leaving any evidence that I had eaten anything else but Sadza and beans, I would wash and put the dishes away before he got home. I was a manikin wife. I didn't feel real or myself. I did as I was told.

Evelyn emphasized that I continue taking contraceptive pills. "Having another child will be like a tsunami," she said.

The issue was Dracul wanted another child. Once again, my sister came to my rescue; she offered to pick up the pills from the local clinic. I devised a way to continue taking contraceptive pills by hiding them in the meal-mealie.

Chapter 12: A Friend

May, three months after my sister and Dracul's fight, he shocked me when with an invitation to come to the city with him on a Saturday. I put on one of the three dresses I was allowed to wear when going out and the one pair of dressy shoes I had. The kind of shoes Beyoncé would put on to go for a walk in her huge back garden.

To my surprise we stopped at his office briefly. I had never been to his work place before.

"Meet my wife Sylvia, Sylvia this is Alice," he said. Alice extended her reddish-brown hand and softly shook my hand.

"How are you?" she said.

"Fine thanks." I lied as I always did.

She wore red heels and a red flared skirt accentuating her curves and a black cotton blouse. Her thick nude lips were the first thing I noticed when I looked at her face.

His office was in a bookstore. It smelled like newly printed bank notes with dim lighting enough to read. "My office is in the back of the bookstore," he said walking through wide aisles with wooden bookshelves on each side.

Browsing a book I picked up from the shelf while I waited for Dracul, Alice approached me.

"I have heard a lot of things about you. Unfortunately, sad things," she whispered looking over her shoulder. "I am sorry to say, but your husband is a jerk. He brags every time he beats you up and says he is your master."

According to the African tradition, women cannot be considered equal to men because of African cultural norms. Obviously, this had been ingrained in Dracul, hence calling himself my master. I must admit that a lot has changed since. A lot of Zimbabweans are defying longstanding beliefs.

Her words felt like a punch in the stomach making me gasp for air. Immediately I became aware of the sound of passing cars and footsteps of people walking in and out of the bookshop.

"My young sister is same age as you, you don't deserve it," she added.

"Thanks for letting me know," I said. At that moment Dracul returned from his office.

I sensed that Alice was genuinely concerned about my situation. On our way out, I made eye contact with her and said, "Nice meeting you." She just smiled.

We returned home that afternoon and Dracul suggested that he wanted to go and apologize to Evelyn about what happened and wanted to make things better. We visited Evelyn the following day, and she accepted his apology. Once again she was allowed to visit me and vice versa.

Taking advantage of Dracul's good mood, and in the hopes of helping us build our marriage, Evelyn suggested that I look for a job. She mentioned that her friend was a manageress for one of the popular clothing stores, Truworths, on First Street in Harare. She offered to find out for me if there were any positions available. She was like a guardian angel, always leading me to better things. To Evelyn and my surprise, Dracul agreed to the idea.

Like Poison Evelyn acted fast. She arranged for my interview for the next day. It was a casual interview. I was offered a position as a cashier. It was my first job ever. In my mind, I believed that having a job would help mend my marriage since I would have an income.

My first day on the job was in June 2nd, 1988. I was paired with Ellen. She had been working at Truworths for over two years and would be by mentor. She came across as nice, bubbly and approachable. My manager couldn't have put me with a better mentor.

My first Saturday I found myself helping Alice. She was surprised to see me behind the counter.

"You work here?" she asked.

"Yeah, this is actually my first week."

"Good for you," she responded. I could feel the happiness in her voice.

My initial impression of Alice was right. She wanted the best for me, and in her eyes, I was like her little sister. We became friends often having lunch together when our schedules permitted. On one such lunch, I confirmed what Dracul bragged about at work, the beatings, cheating and abuse.

"It's your decision but I think you need leave him. You now have a job so at least you have somewhere to start from," she said through a mouthful of her cheese sandwich.

It was end of my first month on a Saturday. The manageress called me into the office and handed me a sealed envelope. I went to the break room and opened it; it was my wages. I felt wide awake as I counted the money. "Wow! I can't believe this is my money," I muttered to myself putting the envelope in my purse. I was so excited to finally have my own money, so I thought.

My mood was crushed when Dracul demanded that I hand over the money that evening. Rubbing my upper arms, I started pacing up and down the room, "Why should I?" I asked. This ruffled his feathers.

"You do as I say or you will have no job." He grabbed me by my braids and did what he did best, punched me in the face twice.

"Please stop," I begged him. "I will give you the money," I pleaded. I had no option but to hand over the envelope. I was so angry that I was not able to say a word to Dracul for a week, except yes and no.

While dropping my son at my sister that Monday, I borrowed her concealer to cover the bruise around my eye. It wasn't enough. Ellen was a very observant person; she kept looking at me funny until she finally asked, "What is wrong with your eye?"

"Nothing, why?" I responded, avoiding eye contact with her.

That afternoon I suggested we go to Wimpy's, our favorite fast food restaurant. The sun blazed down from a cloudless cyan sky making the heat unbearable. People were perspiring and the odor that accompanied some could be smelled a mile away. I couldn't wait to get to Wimpy's and get an icy cold soda to relieve the heat. We decided to sit outside. I spotted two men leaving their table that was under the shade. I hurriedly walked to the table to secure it while Ellen went inside to order our food. I always ordered the same things, steak pie and fries.

I tried to chew my food from the right side of my mouth but realized that I was still sore from the punches received the day before.

"Ouch I groaned," sweeping my food with my tongue to the left side of my mouth.

"What it the matter?" asked Ellen.

At that moment, I broke down. Tears started trickling down my cheeks and a sob formed at the base of my throat as I got ready to come out of my closet. I couldn't hide it from her anymore. I was thankful when she moved her chair next to me and leaned in close, because I did not want our coworkers sitting at the next table to hear what I was about to say. She handed me a tissue from her purse.

"On Saturday after work, he demanded that I hand over my wages. When I refused, he beat me up," I told Ellen still sobbing.

She pulled me into a hug and spoke softly in my ear, "I have been in your shoes. I understand. You have a difficult decision to make, and you will know when it's time to put yourself first," she said.

Her breath smelled like mold as she hugged and comforted me. It used to bother me but on this day, it was the last thing on my mind.

"Tomorrow you need to open a bank account so you can put your wages in as soon as you get paid," she advised.

It had not occurred to me that I needed a bank account. I also found out that day that Ellen had been in an abusive relationship. She had a five-year-old daughter who was living with her mother. Her divorce had been finalized a few months ago. I was so glad to be her friend. She was gorgeous with flawless light brown skin and a huge smile. She introduced me to and taught me how to wear make-up. Her make-up was always on point and most men used to hit on her. When we were out, she drew people's attention.

After my conversation with Ellen over lunch, I felt a sudden release of all tension. I felt like the tumor that I had been walking around with on my back had fallen off. I noticed my hands trembling as I bagged customer's items thinking I could leave Dracul.

I didn't leave right away. Concerned what would happen to our son, I stayed a while longer.

Chapter 13: No More

I had been working for three months now and walked to Evelyn's house each morning. This summer morning was not much different. I walked briskly down the tree lined streets, pushing the stroller, headed to my sister's, to drop my baby off before heading to work. There was a glorious sunrise visible through the trees. I felt the gentle breath of a light breeze upon my face. As I walked, the dream that I had had the night before came back to haunt me. It was still so vivid in my mind.

I dreamt that I had arrived home and when I opened my front door, I was standing on pavement in a strange city. I heard clapping and whistling behind me. I turned around and saw that many people had gathered together. I spotted Dracul, in the crowd. I waved at him, turned around and walked through the door, as it slammed shut behind me. I didn't understand what it meant but I thought it must surely have great significance or it would not have remained so vivid a memory; it was so real.

I dropped my son off and walked to bus stop. The bus was full and smelled like diesel fumes and old rubber. I spotted an empty seat at the back. The bus lurched forward almost making me fall. I grabbed the cold metal pole to catch my balance and finally arrived at the empty seat. An older man who wore a long white garment, was sitting next to me. His head was bald shining like aluminum foil. In his right hand he held a wooden walking stick that was anchored between his feet to keep him from falling over. From the way he was dressed, I could tell that he was an Apostolic Faith member and most probably a prophet.

"Good morning," the old man greeted me.

"Morning," I responded.

After a moment, the man said, "Excuse me, do you believe in dreams?"

I scrunched my eyebrows together. and I tried to speak, but no words came out. It felt as though my lips had been sealed shut from the shock of his question. I nodded my head. Still clear, my dream came back to me again.

When it was time for me to get off the bus, he said, "You have a magnificent life ahead of you."

As I walked towards my work place, the clicking sound of my high heels on the sidewalk, didn't distract me from thinking about what the hell had just happened; on the bus and the dream.

Work was different. There I was distracted by a line of irritated shoppers taking advantage of the end of summer sale. They glanced at their watches frequently, shifting uncomfortably in their positions, scowling at the cashiers. The lines were long but every 'ching, ching' of the cash register came with a slow smile from the next customer.

I smelled french fries and noticed that the next customer was carrying a Chicken Inn box. My stomach started gurgling and rumbling, reminding me it must be close to lunch time. I peeked at the antique clock on the wall behind me and it showed 2:15pm; well past my usual break time. *"Damn I am starving,"* I thought. I had worked through lunch but my supervisor was kind enough to let me go home early that day.

As if my day hadn't been hectic enough, I received a call from Dracul informing me that he was picking me up from work. I told him not to worry; I was knocking off early that day. I walked to the bus station making a mental note to pick a few items from the grocery store. I hadn't mentioned this to Dracul and he would be furious if I was late. This was before cell phones, Facebook or Instagram so I wasn't able to let him know I'd be late.

I spotted my brother-in-law Jacob and his friend standing in the line for the bus. From a distance, I could see why people always thought they were brothers; they were short, fat and round. They looked just like Tweedle Dee and Tweedle Dum. Cutting the line, I casually stood between Jacob and a guy who was third in line. Mind you cutting the line usually got you into trouble, however that day I was lucky, no one said anything. The other guy didn't seem to notice as he was engaged in passionate conversation about a topic he was excited about; he spoke with both, his mouth and hands. Every time he raised his arms, the stench that emanated from his armpits was so foul it would send a skunk running. The bus station was stuffed tighter than a Thanksgiving turkey so there was no place for me to escape the odor. Jacob seemed non-plussed as he discussed politics with his friend. After half an hour, the long awaited ZUPCO bus's front wheels began moving towards us.

I got off at my sister's home to pick my son up. My sister told me that my ex-husband had already picked him.

"Your madman appeared to be in a bad mood. I wonder what is up with him?" she asked.

We talked as she walked me half way home before turning back to her house. I got home and placed the grocery bags on the patterned acrylic blue and white kitchen table in the middle of the room. I smelled alcohol then noticed two empty bottles of lager on the table. I could hear my son trying to imitate a whir sound of a car as he played with his toy car. I kicked my shoes off and walked into the living room where Dracul was sitting on the brown leather couch watching television. Barefooted, the thick carpet felt like I was having the world's best foot massage; my son was sitting on the carpet.

"Hello Hun," I said to my husband. He ignored me.

I picked up my son. I had missed him all day. As I held my son, I remembered what my sister had said earlier, about Dracul being upset. I started wondering what I had done wrong. It did not occur to me that he was furious because I got home way later than he expected. I had proof of where I had been — the groceries. He should understand; so I thought. I knew this was going to be another beating from the look on his face.

I felt the world tilt around me as I stood at the kitchen window wondering what was in store for me at his hands. I knew it was coming I just didn't know when. I forced myself to cook dinner, hoping to avoid escalating his anger. It was quiet in the house except for the television and the sound of sizzling beef on the stove. He was short tempered, finicky, picky, hyper-sensitive over little things. I had to tip-toe around him constantly to prevent angering him. He was the kind of a guy you didn't want to piss off or meet in a dark alley.

I took his plate to him and he said he was not hungry. Well I was starving and sat on the chair with a plate of food on my lap.

"Why did you tell me not to pick you up?" he asked as I started to eat. "If you think that I have beaten you hard before, today I am going to beat the hell out of you and you will tell me who you were with."

In a split second, something incredible happened. I spoke up. With a shaky voice, I said, "Please do not beat me up, let me pack my stuff and leave." At that moment, I wanted him out of my life, like a fart—better out than in. I was sure he really meant it; his eyes were as wide as a tarsier's showing the whites; feet were planted wide apart. I believed he thought I was just saying that.

"Fine with me pack your stuff and leave my son. Go to whoever you were with. He can have you," he responded in a guttural voice.

Still trembling, I walked to the bedroom and started shoving clothes into a suitcase, watching my back at the same time. Tears started trickling down my cheeks. I did not want to cry, but could not stop the tears. The smell of lager in the room let me know he was standing right there.

My mind was now racing; leave the clothes and get out before he does some damage. He was standing there with a bottle of Castle Lager in his right hand. Looking at him was like exchanging stares with a statue. I wiped my eyes on my blouse; I did not want him to see that I was crying in case it ticked him off. I threw more clothes into the suitcase as fast as I could, and dashed out of the house. I still could not believe he was letting me go without giving me a good hiding.

Before I got to the gate, I heard, "Hey!" I turned around, and he was walking towards me with my son in his arms. "Take him with you. He is probably not mine." I reached for my baby, and he said, "Go back inside and get his clothes because once you leave, you are not coming back." Leaving the suitcase by the gate, I went back inside and packed my son's clothes.

Fortunately, my brother-in-law's friend who was at the bus stop with me, lived down the street. I asked him for help with the suitcases. He returned to the house with me and tried to talk to Dracul. He was corroborating my story that I was indeed at the supermarket and that I got on the same bus with him and my brother-in-law, Jacob, and got off at my sister's place to pick up my son. Dracul was standing in the back garden. As we got closer to him, the smell of marijuana got stronger and stronger. He was not interested in talking, my instinct kicked in again, just go.

I went to my pillar of strength—my sister Evelyn. She opened the door and gasped at my puffy face, red eyes and sniffing. "Oooh, dear!" she paused, "Did he beat you again? Is everything alright?" she finished, reaching for my suitcase.

Sobbing I said, "S-Sis… I have left him! I am so done now. I can't take it anymore." Swallowing some of my salty tears I continued, "No he did not beat me. I told him I was leaving him when he threatened to beat me up."

Voices of Abuse

February 7, 2017

Hi Sylvia. Ufunge (I think) you are God send. I am also a victim of domestic violence. It happened six years ago. I am partially healed from it. There are a few people who know my story but they do not know how it affected me. I would be happy to tell you my story.

January 31, 2017

This is a very good book. I was also a victim of domestic violence for many years but 5 years ago I walked out and never looked back.

January 23, 2017

Thank you Tete (Aunt) for inspiring others & enabling them to see the light at the end of the tunnel

January 22, 2017

Well done I walked away 18 years ago in Zimbabwe where you never get help, lost a friend and a cousin from domestic violence. You feel ashamed and because of other people who are not happy and going through domestic violence saying –

You are weak- don't leave – think of the kids. Two happy homes are better than one unhappy home.

January 22, 2017

I am in a domestic violence shelter right now. It's a very important story to tell.

January 21, 2017

Remember, you are your sister's keeper.

February 8, 2017 (conversation with a friend)

Thanks for sharing your story. Domestic abuse happens everywhere. I remember when I was in Zimbabwe, my neighbor was being beaten almost every night by her husband. He would come home drunk and start an argument which led to the beatings. I could hear her screaming and crying so loud. Her kids would also cry. None of the neighbors would help her. I could also hear her head being banged against the wall. The beatings should have been enough to send her away but she never left. I remember one day after the routine beatings of this woman, my maid and I thought she was leaving. Guess what? She stayed. Calling the police in Zimbabwe for a woman who is being beaten is like looking for a needle in the haystack. We tried to offer help but it seemed it was falling on deaf ears. I hope that this woman is still alive.

February 8, 2017

The psychological and emotional abuse was so severe that I did not recognize the face I was looking at in the mirror. The only way that I could feel better was if I harmed myself and feel that pain. I was not allowed to talk to anyone including my family. I was not allowed to voice my opinion, laugh or cry so I buried my emotions.

February 7, 2017

Hi, Sylvia thank you so much, I look forward to reading your book. I lost my sister in 2013 to domestic violence. She was killed by her husband in Zambia.

February 2017

My partner was someone I knew from a while back but we were dating other people then. When those relationships failed, years later we reconnected and started dating. I was at a stage that I realized I did not want to continue with the relationship. He was always angry and was a habitual liar. I suggested we part ways but he called my aunt and everyone thought it was pregnancy hormones running riot. I persisted and he stayed until our daughter was born. When our daughter was six months old I put the pressure for him to leave. He said he wanted to take us to dinner. After dinner, we got home and he started beating me at the car park of my flat. He said he wanted to show me that I was not special because I was too proud. When I made noise, he took me into the house and beat me in front of my other daughter, who was 10 at the time and in front of our baby. He used whatever he could pick up in the house, even the landline handset. He beat me continuously between 9pm to about 6am the next morning and left with my car. He only brought it back a day later at which point all his things were packed and my brothers escorted him to his parents' house. That ended the relationship.

FROM A SOCIAL MEDIA GROUP 01/31/2017

Today we take a minute of silence to remember our sister who was murdered by her husband yesterday 01/30/2017. We will always remember you.......... And all sisters who did not make it. Our thought and prayers are her children she has left behind. May God give them comfort during this terrible time as they grieve for the loss of not one but both parents to such a vicious crime? May her soul rest in peace #domesticviolenceisREAL

Resources

- HTTP://WWW.CRISISTEXTLINE.ORG/
  TEXTLINE/?GCLID=CJWKEAIAOOVE
  BRDD25UYU9LG9YCSJAD0CNBYLTK
  MCUW_2JAHA3GXOEARO3DVIEO0B5
  9MJ59OH8PUSBOC36PW_WCB

  TEXT "CONNECT" TO 741741

- How to find a domestic violence help shelter near you

  https://www.domesticshelters.org/?gclid=CjwKEAi
  AoOvEBRDD25uyu9Lg9ycSJAD0cnBy3h5ws9p9l
  O9A8_tRPs7dlgs4TH6tJLeQA60Hl5vZ8RoCj3Lw
  _wcB

- National Domestic Violence Hotline
  24/7 hotline at 1800-799-7233

  www.the**hotline**.org/

- http://www.rainn.org/
  The Rape, Abuse & Incest National Network
  (RAINN) is the nation's largest anti-sexual assault
  organization. Among its programs, RAINN created
  and operates the National Sexual Assault Hotline at

1.800.656.HOPE and the National Sexual Assault *Online* Hotline at rainn.org . This nationwide partnership of more than 1,100 local rape crisis centers provides victims of sexual assault with free, confidential services, 24 hours per day, 7 days per week. These hotlines have helped over 1.3 million people since RAINN's founding in 1994.

1-800-656-HOPE

National Organizations

- Family Violence Prevention Fund
  383 Rhode Island Street, Suite 304
  San Francisco, CA 94103-5133
  Phone: 415-252-8900
  TTY:800-595-4889
  FAX: 415-252-8991
  E-mail: info@endabuse.org

- *Washington, DC Office*
  1101 14th Street, NW #300
  Washington DC 11005
  Phone: 202-682-1212
  Fax: 202-682-4662

- *Boston Office*
  67 Newbury Street, Mezzanine Level
  Boston, MA 02116
  Phone: 617-262-5900
  Fax:617-262-5901

-
  Lincoln Street
  Suite 1603
  Denver, CO 80203
  Phone: 303 839 1852

TTY: (303) 839-8459
Fax: (303) 831-9251
E-mail: mainoffice@ncadv.org

- Public Policy Office
1633 Q Street NW, Suite 210
Washington, DC 11009
Phone: (202) 745-1211
TTY: (202) 745-2042
Fax: (202) 745-0088
E-mail: publicpolicy@ncadv.org

- National Battered Women's Law Project
275 7th Avenue, Suite 1206
New York, NY 10001
Phone: 212-741-9480
FAX: 212-741-6438

- Safe Horizons
2 Lafayette Street, 3rd Floor
New York, NY 10007
Crime Victims HOTLINE: 800-621-4673
Rape and Sexual Assault & Incest HOTLINE: 212-227-3000
TYY (for all HOTLINES) 866-604-5350
Fax:212-577-3897
E-mail: help@safehorizons.org

- Domestic Violence Shelter Tour
2 Lafayette Street 3rd Floor
New York, NY 10007
Phone: 212-577-7700
Fax: 212-385-0331
24-hour hotline: 800-621-HOPE (4673)

- National Resource Center on Domestic Violence
  Pennsylvania Coalition Against Domestic Violence
  6400 Flank Drive, Suite 1300
  Harrisburg, PA 17112
  Phone: 800-537-2238
  Fax: 717-545-9456

  Legal Office:
  Phone: 717-545-6400
  TOLL FREE: 800-932-4632
  TTY:800-533-2508
  Fax: 717-671-5542

- National Resource Center on Domestic Violence
  Phone: 800-537-2238
  TTY:888-Rx-ABUSE; 800- 595 -4889
  Fax: 717-545-9456

- Health Resource Center on Domestic Violence
  Family Violence Prevention Fund
  383 Rhode Island Street, Suite 304
  San Francisco, CA 94103-5133
  Phone: 800-313-1310
  FAX: 415-252-8991

- Battered Women's Justice Project
  Minnesota Program Development, Inc
  1801 Nicollet Ave, Suite 102
  Minneapolis, MN 55403
  Phone: 800-903-0111, ext.1
  Phone: 612-824-8768
  Fax: 612-824-8965

- Resource Center on Domestic Violence, Child
  Protection, and Custody
  NCJFCJ

P.O. Box 8970
Reno, NV 89507
Office: 775-784-6012
Phone: 800-527-3223
Fax: 775-784-6628
Email: staff@ncjfcj.org
They are only a resource center for professionals and agencies.

- Battered Women's Justice Project
c/o National Clearinghouse for the Defense of
Battered Women
125 South 9th Street, Suite 302
Philadelphia, PA 19107
TOLL-FREE: 800-903-0111 ext. 3
Phone: 215-351-0010
FAX: 215-351-0779
National Clearinghouse is a national resource and advocacy center providing assistance to women defendants, their defense attorneys, and other members of their defense teams in an effort to insure justice for battered women charged with crimes.

- National Clearinghouse on Marital and Date Rape
2325 Oak Street
Berkeley, CA 94708
Phone: 510-524-1582

- Faith Trust Institute
(Formerly Center for the Prevention of Sexual and
Domestic Violence)
2400 N. 45th Street #10
Seattle , WA 98103
Phone: 206-634-1903, ext. 10

Fax: 206-634-0115
Email: info@faithtrustinstitute.org

- National Network to End Domestic Violence
  1101 S Street NW, Suite 400
  Washington, DC 11009
  Phone: 202-543-5566
  HOTLINE:800-799-SAFE (7233)
  TTY: 800-787-3224
  FAX: 202-543-5626

Other Helpful Sites:

- Womenspace National Network to End Violence
  Against Immigrant Women
  1212 Stuyvesant Ave.
  Trenton, NJ 08618
  Phone: 609-394-0136
  24 Hour Mercer County Hotline: 609-394-9000
  Fax:609-396-1093
  Email: info@womenspace.org

- *Counselling & Support Services*
  1860 Brunswick Ave.
  Lawrenceville, NJ 086448
  Phone: 609-394-2532 [1]

I wanted to include resources for Zimbabwe but unfortunately there were very few. However, here are the ones I was able to find. It's a start.

Two Organizations in Zimbabwe

Musasa Project http://www.womeninandbeyond.org/?p=15738

Zimbabwe Women's Lawyers Association (ZWLA)

http://www.zwla.co.zw/index.php/about-us

---

[1] All national resources were gathered from the Feminist Majority Foundation website; www.feminist.org

Made in the USA
San Bernardino, CA
03 March 2017